Fishing Florida's Space Coast:
An Angler's Guide

Ponce de Leon Inlet to Sebastian Inlet

by Capt. John Kumiski

Argonaut Publishing Company
Chuluota, FL

On the cover (clockwise, from top left): Paul Hobby with a big Indian River Lagoon snook; an angler watches from an Indian River Lagoon flat as the Space Shuttle blasts its way into the heavens ; John Kumiski with a beach tarpon; Alex (at right) and Maxx Kumiski with a nearshore cobia; and Barry Kent with a Mosquito Lagoon seatrout. Photo of Barry Kent courtesy of Barry Kent. All other photos by John A. Kumiski.

Cover design by Barry Kent, Kent Advertising Inc., 352.751.0966; kentads@mpinet.net.

Fishing Florida's Space Coast: An Angler's Guide- Ponce de Leon Inlet to Sebastian Inlet
BY CAPTAIN JOHN A. KUMISKI

Published by:
  Argonaut Publishing Company
  284 Clearview Road
  Chuluota, FL 32766 U.S.A.

Copyright ©2003 by John A. Kumiski
First printing 2003
Printed in the United States of America

Publisher's Cataloging in Publication Data
Kumiski, John A., 1952-
   Fishing the Space Coast- An Angler's Guide- Ponce de Leon Inlet to Sebastian Inlet / by
      John A. Kumiski.
   p. cm.

Preassigned LCCN:
ISBN: 0-9635118-0-7 (softcover) $19.95

   1. Saltwater fishing--Florida--Guidebooks. 2. Florida-- Guidebooks. I. Title.

WARNING-DISCLAIMER

This book is designed to provide information in regard to the subject matter covered. It is not, and was never intended to be, a substitute for good judgment or common sense. The reader ventures into or onto the water at his or her own risk.

Every effort has been made to make this book as complete and as accurate as possible. However, there may be mistakes both typographical and in content. Therefore, this book should be used only as a general guide and not as the ultimate source of boating or fishing information.

The purpose of this book is to educate and entertain. The author and Argonaut Publishing Company shall have neither liability nor responsibility to any person with any loss or damage caused, or alleged to be caused, directly or indirectly by the information contained in this book.

If you do not wish to be bound by the above, you may return this book to the publisher for a full refund.

Fishing the Space Coast: An Angler's Guide
Ponce de Leon Inlet to Sebastian Inlet

Table of Contents

About the Author

Capt. John Kumiski is a U.S. Coast Guard licensed captain and fly/light tackle fishing guide based in central Florida's Merritt Island National Wildlife Refuge and Canaveral National Seashore. He has lived in Florida since 1984 and has been guiding for fourteen years. At the time of this writing he is professionally associated with Redington Fly Rods, Cape Fear Fishing Rods, Power Pro Fishing Lines, and DOA Lures.

Kumiski has been fishing since childhood, and fly fishing since his early teens. He is a member of and holds a flycasting instructor certification from the Federation of Fly Fishers, is currently president of the Indian River Guide Association, is a two term past president of the Backcountry Flyfishing Association of Altamonte Springs, and also belongs to the Coastal Conservation Association of Florida, the Florida Outdoor Writers Association, the Southeast Outdoor Press Association, and the Outdoor Writers Association of America. He organizes an annual Fishing Day for Kids through the Backcountry Flyfishing Association, and teaches classes about various types of fishing at Brevard Community College in Cocoa, Florida.

A columnist for Saltwater Fly Fishing magazine and the Fly Fishing Editor for Coastal Angler Magazine, John has contributed hundreds of articles and thousands of photos to many magazines including Florida Sportsman, Sport Fishing, Tide, Fly Rod and Reel, Florida Game and Fish, The Fisherman, and many others, and is the author of four other books, including Flyfishing for Redfish- The Complete Guide to Catching Red Drum on Flies and Flyrodding Florida Salt- How and Where to Catch Saltwater Fish on Flies in the Sunshine State. Kumiski frequently gives fishing seminars and speaks at fishing shows and clubs throughout the Southeast.

Kumiski is 50 years old and is married with two sons. In addition to fishing he enjoys travel, nature study, hiking, paddle sports, camping, mountain biking, photography, reading, writing, and spending quality time with his family.

About the Photos

The aerial photos in this book were taken by the US Geologic Survey, and as such are public domain. If you are wired to the internet you can download these or any other aerial photos of anywhere in North America at almost any resolution you want at www.terraserver.com. This is a tremendous resource for anglers, and makes a fine supplement to this text.

I was as logical as I could be, within the constraints of the equipment used, in my photo selection. I understand that some of the photos are not as helpful as others. www.terraserver.com can give you photos with the resolution you need to explore some of the more out-of-the-way places described in this text.

Introduction

Dear Reader,

This book was meant to be <u>used</u>, not just read. You picked up this book because you need information about fishing along Florida's Space Coast: what tackle to use, how to rig that tackle, what lures and baits are effective. You need to know what techniques work, and which ones do not. You need to know, probably more than anything else, where to go to find those great saltwater gamefish that are so common (some days anyway!) in Space Coast waters.

This book contains all that information, and more! But if it sits on your bookshelf while you're in the boat it can't help you. No, dear reader, this book needs to go fishing with you. Put it in a plastic bag and take it out on the water. Bring a pencil. Scribble in it. Make some notes for future reference. Only by doing this will your money have been well spent.

The book is divided into two sections. The first section has eight chapters that focus on how to fish along the Space Coast. The first chapter discusses tackle, the second baits and lures, the third focuses on presentation, the fourth discusses boats and wading, the fifth examines guides and personal hazards and safety, and the sixth takes a look at fly fishing along the Space Coast. The seventh examines nearshore fishing opportunities and tactics, and the eighth discusses how seasonal changes affect the fish.

The second section describes where to fish. This detailed where-to information is complete with aerial photographs and interviews with some of the Space Coast's top guides (see the next page). These guides shared information on access, types of fishing available, best times of the year, favorite spots and techniques, and a great deal of little known how-to information.

The Space Coast covers about 90 linear miles, from Ponce De Leon Inlet to Sebastian Inlet, with Atlantic and lagoon shorelines, plus numerous canals. No one individual could possibly know it all, and no single book could possibly cover every inch of it. What I have tried to do is to pinpoint easily available, and sometimes not well known, fishing opportunities along the Space Coast. I want anyone to be able to visit this part of Florida with or without a boat, tackle in hand, and find an hour, or a day, or a week, or a lifetime of quality fishing.

So use the book, and let me know how it helps you. I welcome your corrections, comments, criticism, and of course praise, too! I love good news, especially when I helped make it happen! Call me at (407) 977-5207, or email me at spottedtail@spottedtail.com.

Good luck fishing in the Space Coast's great saltwater venues!

Your fishing buddy,

Captain John A. Kumiski

About the Guides, and other Acknowledgements

This book would never have happened without the help and selfless sharing from some of the best guides (and nicest people!) along the Space Coast.

Capt. Eric Davis lives in Sebastian and guides anglers, especially fly casters, in the southern region of the Space Coast, focusing on the area from Sebastian Inlet to Vero Beach. Eric owns The Back Country in Vero Beach, one of the finer fly shops on Florida's east coast. Eric can be reached at 772-567.6665, or through the shop's website at www.verobackcountry.com.

Capt. Tony DeMao lives in Palm Bay. A lifelong Florida resident, Tony also guides in the southern coverage area of this book. Tony can be reached at 321.723.5140.

Capt. Kent Gibbens lives in Ormond Beach. Kent has lived in the Daytona area all his life and has fished Volusia and northern Brevard county waters extensively during that time. Kent is Orvis endorsed and can be reached at 386.672.8929, or through his website: www.backcountrycaptain.com

Capt. Mike Hakala has lived in New Smyrna Beach for 30 years, and has guided the Volusia and northern Brevard area for the more than ten years. He designs and sells Capt. Mike's Guide Proven Lures, available through his website at www.floridaysfishing.com. Mike can be reached at 386.428.8530 locally, or at 800.368.8340.

Capt Fred Hill lives in Edgewater. Although Fred fishes in Volusia and northern Brevard counties, his first love is for snook fishing out of Chokoloskee. Fred can be reached at 386.428.0011.

Capt. John Kumiski authored this book, and guides in the Mosquito Lagoon and the Indian and Banana River Lagoons, as well as doing some nearshore work out of Port Canaveral. He can be reached at 407.977.5207, or via his website at www.spottedtail.com.

Capt. Terry Parsons has lived in Sebastian for more than 30 years. He and his brother own and operate the nearby Wabasso Tackle Shop, 772.589.8518. Terry has been guiding between Grant and Fort Pierce, with emphasis on the Sebastian area, since 1980. Terry can be reached at 772.589.7782.

Capt. Doug Sinclair lives in New Smyrna Beach, where he runs the Saltwater Fly Fishing Academy. Doug guides anglers all around the Volusia county back country, as well as in the Mosquito Lagoon. Doug can be reached at 386.424.1075, or through his website at www.coastalflyfishing.com.

Capt. Rodney Smith is a life long Florida resident who makes his home in Satellite Beach. Rodney guides the Banana River, as well as the nearshore Atlantic out of both Port Canaveral and Sebastian Inlet. Rodney also publishes Coastal Angler Magazine, found at shops all through the Space Coast. He can be reached at 321.777.2773, or via his website at www.camirl.com.

Other people who helped on this project include Patrick Phillips, who worked on the aerial photos and proofreading; Ken Shannon, who provided financial support and proofreading; and my peer reviewers, who read the draft text, pointing out errors and providing valuable suggestions. These people are: Eric Davis, Tony DeMao, Kent Gibbens, Mike Hakala, and Russell and Janet Tharin. Many thanks go out to Barry Kent, who once again did my cover design.

Gentlemen, and Janet, you all have my most sincere thanks. Without your cooperation and information this project could never have reached fruition.

The Space Coast

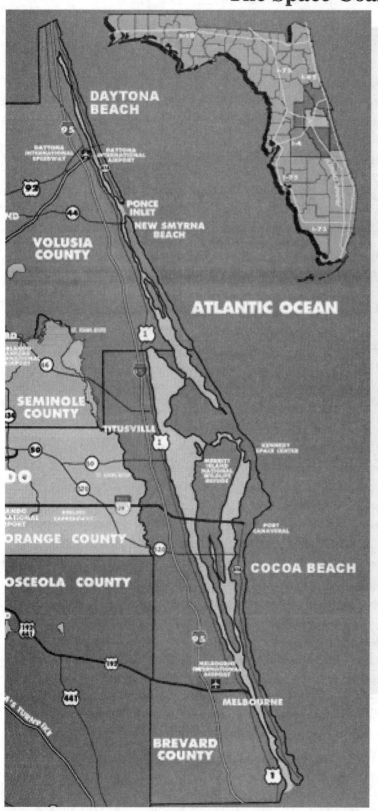

Welcome to Florida's Space Coast.

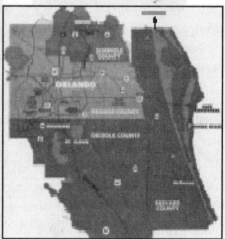

Space Coast
Office of Tourism

8810 Astronaut Blvd. • Suite 102
Cape Canaveral, FL 32920
WWW.SPACE-COAST.COM

1-800-USA-1969
321-868-1126
FAX: 321-868-1139

Map courtesy of Space Coast Office of Tourism.

Chapter 1- Space Coast Fishing Tackle

A Word or Two About Geography

Some unique geography helps explain the world class fishing opportunities available in Space Coast waters. For our purposes the Space Coast will be considered to be between Ponce de Leon Inlet and Sebastian Inlet. From Ponce Inlet all the way to Sebastian Inlet, a barrier island separates the Indian River Lagoon system from the Atlantic Ocean. Other than those two inlets, the only break in this barrier is located at Port Canaveral, where a set of locks prevents tidal influx into the Banana River Lagoon. So this section of the lagoon system, about 90 miles long, has tidal flushing only at either end. Other than at those two inlets, the lagoon system is completely landlocked.

For the most part, this section of the lagoon system is completely tide free. Fishing in this portion of the lagoon system resembles fishing in a large freshwater pond, at least as far as water movement and water levels are concerned.

And just what is this "lagoon system"?

The Indian River Lagoon system, 156 miles long, consists of the Indian River Lagoon, the Mosquito Lagoon, and the Banana River Lagoon. The Mosquito Lagoon lies the farthest north, in Volusia and northern Brevard counties. The northern end of the Indian River Lagoon also lies in Volusia county, but extends south all the way to St. Lucie County, where it ends at the St. Lucie Inlet. This book only covers the section in Volusia and Brevard counties. Lastly, the Banana River Lagoon lies entirely within Brevard county.

The lagoon system is the most ecologically diverse estuary in North America, and harbors over 100 species of fish. For our purposes relatively few of those are important. Red drum, black drum, spotted seatrout, snook, tarpon, jack crevalle, ladyfish, mangrove snapper, and sheepshead are the primary species anglers target in this area. The landlocked feature means that some fish, particularly redfish and seatrout, stay in some portions of the lagoon system for their entire lives. The Space Coast offers the finest shallow water sight fishing opportunities for big redfish anywhere in the universe.

The beach along this strip of the Florida coast is fairly feature free, with five exceptions. Exceptions one and two- the inlets themselves, Ponce to the north and Sebastian to the south. Both have a pair of rock jetties, some very heavy tidal flows, and are incredible fish magnets for much of the year.

The next exception- Cape Canaveral, bristling with NASA launch pads that send a steady stream of rockets towards the heavens, juts out into the Atlantic. Shoals off the beach here give ocean going fish plenty of opportunities to herd and trap bait pods.

Another exception- Port Canaveral supports a wide variety of commercial shipping. Rock jetties lie on either side of the Port's entrance and a 40-plus foot deep, buoyed, dredged channel extends from inside the Port out into the Atlantic for four miles. This makes the area around Port another fish magnet for much of the year.

The final exception- from Patrick Air Force Base south to Sebastian Inlet a live worm rock reef runs along the beach, clearly visible and often exposed at low tide. These rocks host a variety of fish, including pompano, sheepshead, whiting, croakers, snook, and many others, and support an outstanding surf fishery.

The Basic Outfit- Rod and Reel

One can effectively use a wide variety of fishing tackle in Space Coast waters, and this statement is especially true of fishing in the Atlantic. Spinning tackle is the most popular choice, but both plug and fly tackle have their devotees. Still, we have to start somewhere, so let's take a look at what we will consider to be our basic fishing outfit.

A light to medium action (8-15 pound test line range) spinning rod about seven feet long will prove quite versatile when matched to a good quality spinning reel that holds 150 yards or more of 10 or 12 pound test monofilament. Such an outfit will handle all seatrout and most red-fish with ease, as well as most snook not living right in structure. Such an outfit will also be appropriate for ladyfish, most jacks, smaller tarpon, Spanish mackerel, and more; in other words, for most fish under 20 pounds and some types that are larger than that. If you intend to target larger fish you'll need a beefier outfit.

Spinning (actually, all) reels need to be of reasonably high quality. Saltwater quickly eats up cheap tackle. A better reel will last longer. Also, some monster fish swim in these waters. If you hook a trophy with a reel that's a piece of junk your chance of landing it is mighty small. If you have to cut corners on tackle quality, cut somewhere else in your system.

Equivalent plug tackle works every bit as well, and possibly more so. When fighting a big fish with plug tackle you won't have problems with line twist that you do with spinning tackle. On the other hand using the plugging outfit takes more time to learn to use, and requires more skill, than using a spinning outfit.

For a complete discussion of fly tackle appropriate for this area see the chapter on fly fishing. Quickly though, an eight-weight outfit with a floating line performs very adequately.

Line

Line likewise is not a place to cut corners on quality. After all, it's what connects you to the fish. You can save some money on line by buying large spools like those quarter pound spools. A quarter pound of good quality monofilament will cost somewhere around 10 dollars.

Nowadays you have some options when it comes to line, though. While monofilament of various kinds is still the most popular line used here, at least two other choices are available. Fluorocarbon lines look like mono but do not absorb water, are not degraded as much by ultra-violet light, and are nearly invisible to fish. They stretch about the same amount as monofilament. Needless to say, fluorocarbon lines cost more than do monofilament lines.

Spectra braids are also available. I feel that Spectra lines have several advantages over monofilament. They do not stretch, and as a result are extremely sensitive. You can feel everything that happens at the business end of your line. Another result of the low stretch is that when you set the hook, the hook gets set. There is no rubber band effect as there is with mono.

Spectra lines are much thinner than mono lines of the same breaking strength. You can use a thinner, stronger line, resulting in both longer casts and fewer break-offs. Spectra lines seem relatively unaffected by line twist. While only one big fish will trash a monofilament line, Spectra lines can be used day after day, month after month, fish after fish. They last far longer than mono lines.

Foot for foot Spectra lines are quite a bit more expensive than mono lines, but they last so much longer that I feel they're actually a much better value. My favorite line is called Power Pro, but some other brands of Spectra lines are also good.

Leaders

You will usually need some kind of leader when fishing in Space Coast waters, regardless of what species you hope to catch. What functions does this leader need to perform?

Your leader creates a (hopefully) nearly invisible connection between the line and your bait. The leader also prevents breakage due to abrasion from sharp teeth, sharp gill plates, rough skin, oysters, barnacles, etc.

It should be obvious that you want a thin leader for invisibility and a thick leader for abrasion resistance. So leader diameter will always be a compromise, and the thickness of your leader usually depends on what type of fish you expect to target. That having been said, by far and away the best material to use for most leaders is fluorocarbon.

Without going into the physics of it, fluorocarbon bends light to nearly the same degree as does water. Their "index of refraction" is almost the same. Fish don't see fluorocarbon very well. It resists abrasion better than does nylon. These two qualities make fluorocarbon the most perfect leader material yet invented.

That having been said, in some situations even fluorocarbon just doesn't cut it. The teeth of king mackerel, barracudas, and sharks all make quick work of most nonmetallic leaders. For these fish you need to use stainless steel wire.

The chart below gives most fish species and the thickness of leader (in pound test) needed.

Fish Species	Recommended Leader Strength (fluorocarbon)
seatrout, redfish, black drum, whiting, pompano, mangrove snapper, little tunny (bonito)	12-15 pound
jack crevalle, bull redfish, flounder, sheepshead	20 pound
snook, baby tarpon (to 20 pounds), ladyfish, big jacks, Spanish mackerel, cobia, tripletail	30-40 pound
midsize tarpon (30-70 pounds)	40-50 pound
large tarpon (over 70 pounds), small sharks	60-80 pound
large sharks, king mackerel, barracuda	#3 or 4 stainless steel wire

You can fudge on these values somewhat. The fish won't read this!

How long should the leader be? Although (again) there are no hard and fast answers, when fishing in the lagoon system I like a leader between two and three feet. I don't carry a net and want to have something to grab onto when the fish is near the boat. One rule of thumb is that the leader length should be a little longer than the largest fish you anticipate catching.

As the leader gets heavier shorter leaders often work better, since a fat knot has trouble passing through the rod's tip-top when casting. You can also step up the leader, something like a fly caster's tapered leader in reverse. For example, when fishing for large tarpon, you could attach a section of 30 pound monofilament to your doubled 20 pound test line, then attach a foot or two of 60 or 80 pound test fluorocarbon to the 30 pound mono. There are no absolute rules to this, so use whatever you find works best for you.

Knots

There are lots of knots you can use. I don't know them all, and you don't need to, either. If you can tie the following five knots well, they will get you though almost any situation except for using wire. Wire use requires a Haywire twist.

Bimini twist

Use this to double the business end of your line where you tie it to your leader. It will give you 100 percent knot strength.. While it looks difficult, it's actually a very easy knot to tie.

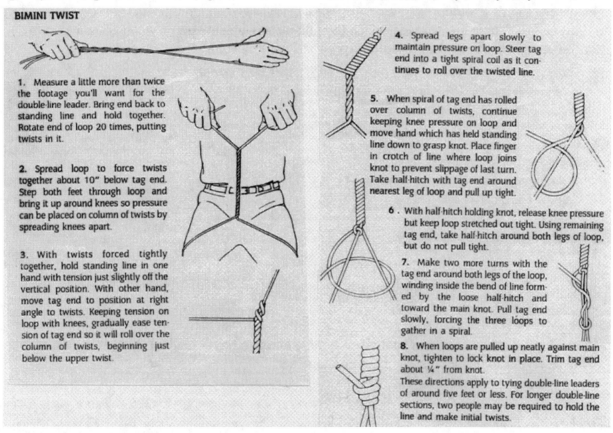

BIMINI TWIST

1. Measure a little more than twice the footage you'll want for the double-line leader. Bring end back to standing line and hold together. Rotate end of loop 20 times, putting twists in it.

2. Spread loop to force twists together about 10" below tag end. Step both feet through loop and bring it up around knees so pressure can be placed on column of twists by spreading knees apart.

3. With twists forced tightly together, hold standing line in one hand with tension just slightly off the vertical position. With other hand, move tag end to position at right angle to twists. Keeping tension on loop with knees, gradually ease tension of tag end so it will roll over the column of twists, beginning just below the upper twist.

4. Spread legs apart slowly to maintain pressure on loop. Steer tag end into a tight spiral coil as it continues to roll over the twisted line.

5. When spiral of tag end has rolled over column of twists, continue keeping knee pressure on loop and move hand which has held standing line down to grasp knot. Place finger in crotch of line where loop joins knot to prevent slippage of last turn. Take half-hitch with tag end around nearest leg of loop and pull up tight.

6. With half-hitch holding knot, release knee pressure but keep loop stretched out tight. Using remaining tag end, take half-hitch around both legs of loop, but do not pull tight.

7. Make two more turns with the tag end around both legs of the loop, winding inside the bend of line formed by the loose half-hitch and toward the main knot. Pull tag end slowly, forcing the three loops to gather in a spiral.

8. When loops are pulled up neatly against main knot, tighten to lock knot in place. Trim tag end about ¼" from knot.
These directions apply to tying double-line leaders of around five feet or less. For longer double-line sections, two people may be required to hold the line and make initial twists.

Albright special

Use this knot to tie line to leader when the two are of dissimilar diameter, or when tying Spectra to other monofilament or fluorocarbon. See the following page.

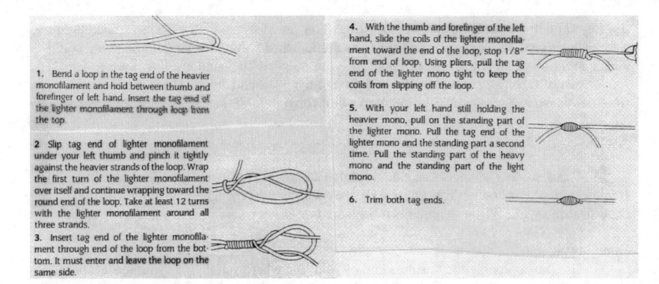

1. Bend a loop in the tag end of the heavier monofilament and hold between thumb and forefinger of left hand. Insert the tag end of the lighter monofilament through loop from the top.

2. Slip tag end of lighter monofilament under your left thumb and pinch it tightly against the heavier strands of the loop. Wrap the first turn of the lighter monofilament over itself and continue wrapping toward the round end of the loop. Take at least 12 turns with the lighter monofilament around all three strands.

3. Insert tag end of the lighter monofilament through end of the loop from the bottom. It must enter and leave the loop on the same side.

4. With the thumb and forefinger of the left hand, slide the coils of the lighter monofilament toward the end of the loop, stop 1/8" from end of loop. Using pliers, pull the tag end of the lighter mono tight to keep the coils from slipping off the loop.

5. With your left hand still holding the heavier mono, pull on the standing part of the lighter mono. Pull the tag end of the lighter mono and the standing part a second time. Pull the standing part of the heavy mono and the standing part of the light mono.

6. Trim both tag ends.

Double Surgeon's knot/loop

Use this to tie line to leader when their diameters are similar, or when tying a loop in the end of a piece of line. Use a triple surgeon's if tying Spectra.

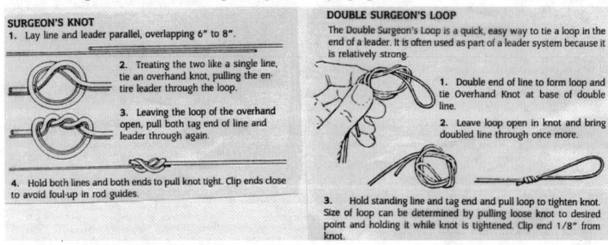

SURGEON'S KNOT

1. Lay line and leader parallel, overlapping 6" to 8".

2. Treating the two like a single line, tie an overhand knot, pulling the entire leader through the loop.

3. Leaving the loop of the overhand open, pull both tag end of line and leader through again.

4. Hold both lines and both ends to pull knot tight. Clip ends close to avoid foul-up in rod guides.

DOUBLE SURGEON'S LOOP

The Double Surgeon's Loop is a quick, easy way to tie a loop in the end of a leader. It is often used as part of a leader system because it is relatively strong.

1. Double end of line to form loop and tie Overhand Knot at base of double line.

2. Leave loop open in knot and bring doubled line through once more.

3. Hold standing line and tag end and pull loop to tighten knot. Size of loop can be determined by pulling loose knot to desired point and holding it while knot is tightened. Clip end 1/8" from knot.

Uni-knot

Use this to make a loop knot when tying a lure to a heavy leader (allows the lure to swing freely) or to tie two pieces of Spectra together.

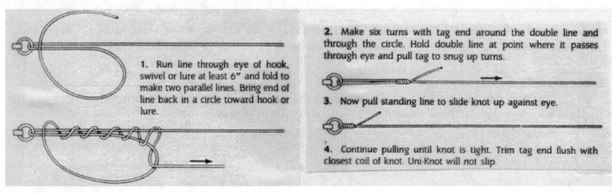

1. Run line through eye of hook, swivel or lure at least 6" and fold to make two parallel lines. Bring end of line back in a circle toward hook or lure.

2. Make six turns with tag end around the double line and through the circle. Hold double line at point where it passes through eye and pull tag to snug up turns.

3. Now pull standing line to slide knot up against eye.

4. Continue pulling until knot is tight. Trim tag end flush with closest coil of knot. Uni-Knot will not slip.

Clinch knot

Use this to tie a hook or lure onto a line or leader. Do not use this with Spectra.

1. An old standby. Pass line through eye of hook, swivel or lure. Double back and make five turns around the standing line. Hold coils in place; thread end of line through first loop above the eye, then through big loop, as shown.

2. Hold tag end and standing line while coils are pulled up. Take care that coils are in spiral, not lapping over each other. Slide tight against eye. Clip tag end.

Haywire twist

Use this to tie a hook or lure onto a piece of single strand, stainless steel wire leader.

1) Gently bend six inches of wire back onto itself. Do not put a kink in it! Twist the wires around each other.

2) When you have six twists in the wire, begin doing "barrel wraps" by twisting the tag end around the main piece of wire. You will need four to six barrel wraps depending on the diameter of the wire. It should look like the illustration below,

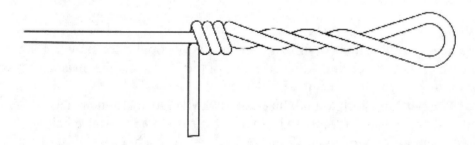

3) After finishing the barrel wraps complete the twist by placing the tag at 90 degrees to the loop. Bend the tag back and forth until it breaks off. If you do this it will not leave a sharp point, important for avoiding cuts when handling the leader. See below.

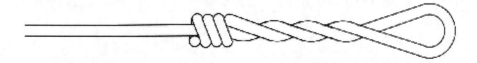

Rigs

Oh yes, we could spend a lot of time here. However, my philosophy requires keeping things simple, so that's what we're going to do.

-Basic Rig

Tie a Bimini twist in the end of the line. Use an Albright to attach about three feet of fluorocarbon leader. Tie the hook or lure to the end of the leader. Go fishing.

If more casting weight is needed (for pitching shrimp, for instance) I just pinch on a split shot right by the hook.

-Egg Sinker Rig

Take a barrel swivel and use a clinch knot to tie it to the end of your line. I recommend doubling the line first with a Bimini twist but this isn't strictly necessary. Take 14 inches or so of leader material (20 to 30 pound test) and tie it to the other side of the swivel, again using a clinch knot.

Take your sinker (weight varies according to conditions) and slide it up the leader, then tie the loose end of the leader to a second barrel swivel. Use clinch knots. The sinker is now secured between the two swivels.

Finally, take a last piece of leader material (length varies according to conditions) and tie it to the second swivel. Tie a hook to the end of the leader and go fishing.

Popping Cork Rig

Get a popping cork and place it about two or three feet above the hook of a basic rig. Popping corks are usually used with bait, but a jig or a DOA Shrimp could be used just as easily and effectively. To use the rig, cast it out where you hope there are some fish. Every 30 or 40 seconds give the line a sharp pull with the rod tip. The cork will pop, making a noise that will attract curious fish. When they come to see what the commotion is, there's your bait.

-Stinger kingfish rig

There are many modifications of this rig, which is very popular for slow trolling menhaden or other baitfish for king mackerel. Adjust the size of the hooks and the distance between them to the size of the bait you'll be using.

Use a haywire twist to attach a small black barrel swivel to an 18 inch piece of #3 wire. To the other end of the wire use a haywire twist to attach a #1/0 to #3/0 bronze bait hook.

Take a second piece of wire about 12 inches long and use a haywire twist to attach it to the eye of the same hook. To the other end of this piece of wire use the haywire twist to attach a # 1 or #2 bronze treble hook. This is the "stinger", and it should be about five or six inches behind the lead hook.

King mackerel often clip a bait in half, swallowing the tail and then circling around to pick up the head. If you're trolling you pull the head away and they can't find it. The stinger hooks these short strikers, allowing you to catch fish you would otherwise only be feeding.

Chapter 2- Baits and Lures for the Space Coast

The word "bait" has several different meanings in fishing. It could mean live or dead fish, worms of various types, shrimp, crabs, clams, etc. It could be generically applied to artificial lures. The word can even be applied to flies. For example, if you tell someone you caught six redfish, they are quite likely to ask, "What kind of bait were you using?" (They'll also want to know where you were fishing, but that's a different story.)

To avoid confusion in this chapter, when the word "bait" is used here it refers to natural bait, alive or dead. "Lure" refers to an artificial fish attracting device made from wood, plastic, and/or metal that is used with conventional tackle. "Fly" refers to a hook with some kind of natural or synthetic fibers attached to it by means of thread, usually used with a fly rod.

Some people fish with nothing but bait. Others use nothing but artificial lures. Still others use nothing but flies. And still others (the most pragmatic types) use whatever is most appropriate at the time, or whatever their mood tells them to use. We are going to look at all the different types of bait, and many different types of lures.

There are no absolutes in fishing. What's presented here are my opinions. I try to be logical and have good reasons for doing things, but feel free to disagree with me. And please, take the time to experiment with your own ideas.

Hooks

In order to use bait you have to have a hook. In Florida most of the time a single hook is required by law to be used for inshore fish- no trebles are allowed with bait for many species. The only exception to a single hook that I can think of is the small treble used as a stinger in a king mackerel rig.

As a general rule you always want to use the smallest hook (and sinker, for that matter) that will get the job done. When it comes to terminal tackle, less is almost always better, since it allows for a more natural presentation of the bait. The wise angler will carry a range of sizes of his favorite hook styles from as small as size 10 (for catching bait like pinfish) to as large as 5/0 (for using that pinfish as bait for tarpon).

In Florida we have strict laws covering the taking of marine fishes (the FWC website where these laws can be checked is www.marinefisheries.org). Bag limits for some popular species are small, one redfish per day, for example. Size limits on many fish are quite strict, with seatrout, redfish, and snook all coming to mind. We have a lot of catch and release fishing. I try to pick my bait hooks with that in mind.

Fish take bait because it looks and smells like food. Consequently it is not at all unusual for them to take the hook deep into their mouth, or even into their esophagus or stomach. If you pull the hook out of a gut hooked fish, that fish is going to die. If you cut the line and leave the hook in the fish it may die anyway, but it might not. At least it's got a chance. Frequently I catch fish that are quite healthy in spite of the fact that they are carrying hooks and sometimes even lures around with them, so at least some of them make it.

I have two favorite bait hooks. One is the Eagle Claw Kahle hook with the bronzed finish, #L141. I use these in sizes 2, 1, 1/0, and 2/0 for any fish up to about 30 pounds or so. The wire is thin so they rust quite readily. I would like to think this helps the deeply hooked fish get rid of them more quickly, but honestly I don't know if this is true or not.

For larger fish I prefer circle hooks. My favorite is the Daiichi Circle Wide in sizes 4/0 through 12/0. While fish can still be gut hooked with circle hooks most of the time this style will catch in their lip. Once this hook is seated it very seldom comes out, making it an especially good hook choice for tarpon.

Bait

Many different kinds of baits present themselves to the fisherman for use. What you need to know is what each is for, how to use it, and how to get it.

-Shrimp

Shrimp are probably the universal bait. By that I mean that almost any fish you're interested in catching will eat them. From my (lazy) perspective the problem with using them is that many fish you have absolutely no interest in catching will eat them, too.

I find them most useful for sight-fishing: that is, casting them into the path of fish that you can see. They are also widely used with a popping cork. You can also use them with an egg sinker rig, but you'll get pecked to death by pinfish, blowfish, catfish, sting rays, etc.

While in some parts of the state shrimp can be castnetted, they are most easily picked up at the local bait shop. Most folks prefer using live shrimp, but fresh dead or frozen ones also work for many species. One good thing about using live shrimp is that the ones you have left over can be taken home and eaten. This is something you probably wouldn't want to do with menhaden or worms.

Hooking Shrimp Through Head or Tail

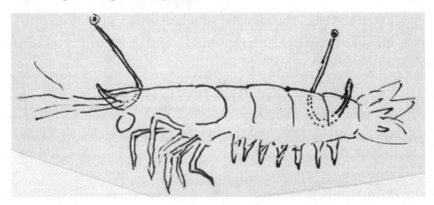

-Crabs

Crabs are somewhat less than a universal bait, but they are absolutely deadly on some species. Fiddler crabs are an excellent and popular bait for sheepshead, but redfish and black drum will also eat them. Those little brown crabs you see on docks and mangrove trees are another excellent bait for big sheepshead, redfish, and black drum.

Mole crabs, more commonly known as sand fleas, are an excellent surf fishing bait for whiting and pompano. Other types of fish may surprise you by taking your flea, too. While these can be purchased frozen at your local bait shop, live ones work much better and are often easy to dig up at the water's edge once you get to the beach.

The swimming crabs, blue crabs and their relatives, are the most popular and widely used crab bait. Large ones can be cut into halves or quarters and used for redfish and black drum. Smaller, silver dollar sized live crabs make superb baits for tarpon, redfish, black drum, and permit (unfortunately rare in Space Coast waters).

Blue crabs have a nasty disposition and mean claws. Handle live individuals that still have those claws with a great deal of care.

Live and frozen blue crabs, as well as live fiddler crabs, are often available at bait shops. You can catch your own bait sized blue crabs with a long handled, fine mesh dip net by walking the shorelines of the lagoon and searching for them. You can often catch fiddlers by hand by doing the same thing in the system's more quiet corners.

Hooking crabs

-Clams

I have only used clams for bait a couple of times. They don't stay on a hook too well. Black drum love them. You can dig your own or buy them in bait shops.

To put them on a hook, first break one open by clapping two together. Pick the meat out of the loser's shell and put it on the hook. Cast gently so you don't lose it!

-Minnows

There are a lot of small fish, and some not so small, that can be used for bait. They can be used alive or dead, whole or in pieces. One great thing about using fish for bait is that you tend not to get the bait stealers bothering you quite as much as with shrimp. Another benefit is that if you have a freezer you can usually keep a supply of effective bait on hand at all times.

Due to space limitations this listing is of necessity incomplete. An excellent reference is

Vic Dunaway's <u>Sport Fish of Florida</u>. Let's take a look at an alphabetical listing of some of the Space Coast's more popular baitfish.

-Croaker. Usually found along the surf, a live croaker is like an ice cream sundae to big snook. For that matter if you get big ones (they get to maybe three pounds) you can eat them yourself. Can be caught with a cast net or by hook and line.

-Killifish, a.k.a. "mud minnows." Small fish (to five inches), can be used alive for redfish, seatrout, tarpon, and snook, but are best known as flounder baits. Catch them with a cast net.

-Ladyfish. A fine light tackle sport fish in their own right, ladyfish make excellent baits for redfish, snook, seatrout, tarpon, and sharks. Small ones can be used whole, alive or dead. Bigger ones can be cut into chunks. Although they get soft, they can be frozen for future use. Usually caught on hook and line, they can sometimes be cast netted in mosquito control canals.

-Menhaden, a.k.a. "pogies." These form huge schools along Space Coast beaches during the summer and are wonderful baits for tarpon, sharks, cobia, king mackerel, redfish, and snook. They can also be found and used in the lagoon. Although they can be chunked they're kind of soft, so are usually used alive. They get too soft to freeze well. I've gotten them on Sabikis, but they're usually cast netted.

-Mojarra. A fine bait for redfish, trout, snook, and tarpon, usually used alive, and usually cast netted incidentally while throwing for mullet.

-Mullet. The big ones are black mullet, the smaller ones are silver mullet. Both make excellent bait for a wide variety of fish, alive or dead, whole or in chunks, fresh or frozen. Mullet are usually cast netted, and are also widely available frozen in bait shops. I even see them in Wal-Mart.

-Pigfish. What sound does a pig make? Pigfish grunt too, calling big trout, redfish, snook, and tarpon right to them. Speaking evolutionarily, it doesn't seem like a trait that would be selected. Anyway, pigfish are always used alive, and unless you run a line of traps they have to be purchased at a bait shop. They're usually only cast netted incidentally, and they are only available during the summer.

-Pilchards. Pilchards, when large enough for the hook, make a wonderful bait for all kinds of fish. They are used alive, and are always cast netted. They are a much more important bait on Florida's west coast than along the Space Coast.

-Pinfish. Pinfish are just as useful a bait fish as mullet, good alive or dead, fresh or frozen, whole or in chunks. You can cast net them, catch them on hook and line, or buy them at bait shops. Be careful handling them. The spines on their fins will puncture your fingers.

-Sand Perch. Mostly found along the beach, sand perch make good baits for snook, tarpon, redfish and more. They can be caught by cast net or hook and line.

-Spot. Spot are, like sand perch and croakers, found along the beach, cast netted or hook and lined, and make good baits for the same species.

-Thread Herring, aka "greenies." Threads get in huge schools along Space Coast beaches where they provide plenty of meals for tarpon, cobia, barracudas, jacks, little tunny, and more. They can be cast netted with a good quality, fast sinking net, or can be caught on a Sabiki rig. Thread herring are usually used alive.

Hooking Methods for Minnows

-Through the Lips

This method can be used for mud minnows, ladyfish, mojarra, mullet, pinfish, and sand perch. Take the hook and drive it through the bottom lip and out through the top lip. Usually with mullet you insert the hook point into their mouth and out through the top lip.

-Through the Nose

This is used for menhaden, pilchards, and thread herring. In front of the eye there is a little hollow. The hook point is inserted in one side of the nose in this hollow, and comes out the other.

When slow trolling menhaden for king mackerel a "stinger" is frequently used. Run a piece of stainless steel leader wire from the nose hook to a small treble that is hooked near the bait's tail. Kings often clip the bait in half, swallowing just the tail section. The stinger will hook fish that do this.

-Through the Back/Tail

You can hook almost any type of minnow behind the dorsal fin. It works well when fishing the bait under a float. For some minnows, such as croaker, spot, mojarra, pinfish, and pigfish, this is the preferred method. Be careful to avoid the fish's backbone when you hook it.

Chunking

Dealing with live bait can be a real pain in the neck. It has to be obtained somehow, and then kept alive. This last is easier if you have a boat with a big live well, but not everyone does.

Live baits often won't stay where you want them, either. You cast them where you want them, and they swim away. Sometimes they are so lively that the target fish try to eat them, miss a few times, and give up. Enter- tatata-DA! the CHUNK.

A chunk is a piece of baitfish, usually a steak but sometimes a fillet. It has several advantages over a live bait. You can catch bait to be chunked at your convenience and then keep it in your freezer until you need it. A chunk never swims away from where you throw it. Cutting chunks can turn a much-too-big bait into several perfectly sized baits.

Many people have asked me about a chunk's effectiveness compared to live bait. Compare the attitude of the fish to your own. Do you want to catch and kill the cow, or do you prefer to have a piece of it served to you hot and sizzling on a platter?

Redfish, seatrout, and sharks take chunks freely. I have caught tarpon and jack crevalle on chunks. And while I've never caught a snook on a chunk, friends in other parts of Florida assure me that they do work well for snook.

When I anchor up to go chunking, I usually put a time limit of 20 to 30 minutes on my attempt. I always pick a spot where I know fish have been recently. If the fish are there I will catch some. If the time limit passes without a bite I go try somewhere else. It's quite simple.

I do not really enjoy still fishing. I find it much more enjoyable to hunt for, stalk, and present my offering to fish I can see. But when weather conditions or the skill level or expectations of my anglers force me to, or when I need a fish for the table, I chunk. It's one of the most effective methods of fishing for redfish that there is.

Artificial Lures

When using bait, you're using the hunger of the fish against it by offering real food. Using lures is generally considered to require more skill than does using bait, since you're trying to fool the fish into striking a piece of wood, plastic, or metal, something that's clearly not very tasty or nutritious.

Although some defy placement, lures are usually classified into several different groups.

-Plugs. Plugs are made of wood or plastic, and generally sport two or more sets of gang hooks. Some float, some sink, and some float at rest but dive on the retrieve. Since so much of our fishing is catch and release, and since plugs have so many hooks, these are my own least favorite type of lure. Many fine anglers I know always press down the barbs of their plug's hooks to facilitate release of caught fish. This can be done with any type of artificial, including flies.

Plugs themselves come in several different categories- poppers/chuggers, rattling plugs, swimming plugs, and many more.

-Spoons. Spoons for saltwater are almost always made of shiny, curved, highly polished metal. Some have a single treble hook, some have one single hook. The spoons with single hooks usually have weedguards, and are among the best lures to use for redfish.

-Jigs. A jig consists of a head that's a piece of metal, usually lead, molded around a hook, and a tail which might be feathers, hair, synthetic fibers, soft plastic, or a combination of two or more of these materials. They are among the most useful and versatile lures you can use. Jigs are often "tipped" with a piece of shrimp to add scent appeal. Sometimes a jig head is used in conjunction with bait, usually a whole live shrimp or small fish like a mullet.

-Soft Plastic Lures. These come in an astonishing variety of sizes, shapes, and colors, and are among the most effective lures available. Some, like the DOA Lure line or Capt. Mike's Guide Proven Lures, come rigged and ready to fish. Other types require the angler to rig them. Like jigs (with which soft plastics are often used) they are incredibly versatile.

An angler looking to put together a starter kit for fishing in Space Coast waters needs a variety of lures that can cover the entire water column, from the surface to the bottom. I have learned that it's usually better to have several of each lure that you know works than a wide variety of stuff that just attracted your eye. The following chart offers guidelines.

Lure Recommendations for Space Coast Waters

Lure Type	Uses
Surface Plug (popper/ chugger, stick bait)	Blind casting over flats or in the ocean, especially when surface activity is observed. Excellent choice for jack crevalle, seatrout, snook, little tunny. I don't like plugs but there is no substitute for a popper sometimes. Popular choices in surface plugs include the venerable Zara Spook, the MirroLure Top Dog series, and the Chug Bug from Storm. There are many other good ones. Disadvantages- hooks hang up on floating grass/weed, and make unhooking fish very difficult sometimes unless barbs are pressed.
Spoon	A 1/4 ounce weedless spoon in gold or silver is a must in every lagoon fisherman's kit, especially for redfish. Captain Mike's is a popular style. The Gator spoon has long been a standard for ocean-going bluefish. A spoon-like lure called a Sting Silver can be very useful in the ocean for mackerel and little tunny.
Jigs (1/8th ounce and up)	Jigs will take every species of gamefish in Florida waters. A variety of weights need to be carried to accommodate changing depth and current conditions. For maximum versatility get jig heads without tails and use these with a variety of soft plastic tails. RipTide markets a weedless jighead that is extremely useful when used on grass flats.
Soft Plastics	An entire book could be written about using various soft plastic baits. You need to carry some to be used with jig heads (curly tails, grubs, and shad tails). You'll also need some twitch baits (Capt. Mike's Flats Candy 2, Bass Assassin, Sluggo, Jerk Worm, etc.). There are some plug-like soft plastics with single hooks that are excellent- the DOA Lure line (especially the Bait Buster, Shrimp, and TerrorEyz) comes to mind. Soft plastic lures can be used to catch every kind of gamefish that swims in Florida waters.

Chapter 3- Presenting the Bait/Lure

We may be putting the cart before the horse here, since ordinarily finding the fish is a prerequisite to presenting the bait. But since the entire second section of this book is dedicated to finding the fish, for the moment we will assume that the finding problem has been solved.

The casual observer may not believe this, but fish have moods. Some days they act extremely aggressively and will strike almost anything. Some days they won't eat at all, or let anglers in a boat anywhere near them. It can be very frustrating when they act like this, but that's fishing. Anyone who tells you they always catch fish is a stereotypical fisherman. In other words, they're lying.

Compared to mammals, fish have very small brains. Fish are stupid, and are probably incapable of thought as we understand it. However, they are capable of learning and they are very good at staying alive. Most Space Coast fish have learned what boats are, and associate them with trouble. This is especially true on the shallow flats of the lagoon system.

It cannot be stressed strongly enough how important it is to be quiet when stalking flats fish. The grinding of the pushpole on the bottom will spook them. The turning propeller of an electric motor will spook them, especially if it's turning fast or changing speeds. Any movement of people's feet in the boat, especially what I call "clomping," will cause a fish stampede. If you want to catch fish in shallow water you had better be extremely quiet.

Presentations When Sight Fishing on the Flats

Space Coast flats fish have learned that a big "plop" anywhere near them is bad news. If you want to scare fish on the flats, hit them right behind the head with a nice juicy mullet chunk. Heck, flies put to close to redfish, snook, and trout scare them when they're on the flats, never mind something that hits the water like a boulder.

Another presentation that will usually spook flats fish is the "attacking lure." A common presentation error is casting past the fish and drawing the lure towards it. Fish aren't usually attacked by their prey, and in Space Coast waters they will seldom stand for it.

This book is incapable of describing every possible situation that you might encounter. Flats fish lay up, tail, fin out, or cruise at varying rates of speed. They might be singles, in small groups, or be in a school containing hundreds of individuals. They might be redfish, black drum, jack crevalle, seatrout, snook, tarpon, or one of the other less frequently encountered species. They might be stationary, or moving at a high rate of speed.

Regardless of what kind of fish it is, though, most have what we can call a "strike zone." A strike zone is an area around the head of the fish where, if the bait or lure is placed with skill, the fish will take it. Strike zones are almost always in front of the fish, and in their path of travel. The farther you ask the fish to move to take whatever it is you are offering, the less likely they are to take it.

Some fish are designed to feed above. Snook, seatrout, jacks, and tarpon all have protruding lower jaws. Their mouths point up. They are more likely to take a lure that is higher in the water column than they are, or take it off the surface.

Other fish are designed to feed down. Redfish and black drum have overbites, and tail as they feed on the bottom. Your offering being below them won't bother them at all.

So, your challenge as an angler is to place your offering out in front of the fish, leave it there until the fish is close enough to see it, and then manipulate that offering so that the fish will see it and eat it.

I tell all my anglers to try to anticipate where the fish is going and put their offering there. This is usually easier said than done, even for big groups of fish. The tendency of most fishermen is to cast to the fish, or to a swirl where the fish was a moment ago.

In order to make a cast to where the fish is going, you have to be able to see the fish and determine its speed and direction of movement. Then you have to make a cast that lands far enough in front of the fish that it doesn't spook, but close enough that it's able to see your offering. The farther ahead you lead the fish, the more likely it is to change directions, not go where you cast, and never see your offering. Sight casting is a challenging game.

If you're fishing with bait, you can cast your offering in front of the fish and just leave it there. They will see and/or smell it. If they are at all on the feed one of them will usually pick it up. If you're throwing to a single this still holds true, but your target area is much smaller, since you have to put the bait into the strike zone of that individual.

If you're casting a lure or fly, the same approach usually works. Cast your lure in front of the fish and leave it there until you think the fish is close enough to see it. Then, and only then, start to move it. The approaching fish perceives that its approach spooked something that's now trying to get away, a response it sees from its prey all the time. The usual reaction of the fish is to take your offering.

Now of course bad casts will be made. The possibilities are, you hit the fish (very bad), land behind it/them (works less than one percent of the time), land too far in front, too far past it, or not far enough. When this happens a quick evaluation needs to be made. Will the cast work? Is there a reasonably good possibility that the fish will go where your offering is? If so, leave it there! If not, reel like mad and make another, better cast. But remember that patience often turns a less than perfect cast into one that will work.

Casts that are too long can often be saved without reeling the bait/lure into the fish and spooking it. Start reeling before the bait/lure hits the water. Hold the rod high and reel fast enough that the bait/lure stays on the surface, where you can see it (very important!). When it gets to the place you want, stop reeling and let it sink.

This approach will still spook fish, but nowhere near as often as a conventional retrieve. This also works well for fish that are tailing, or laid-up fish. More than once I've had a fish I didn't know was there blow up on a bait that I was skimming across the surface, intending to put it in front of another fish that I could see. Needless to say, this is very surprising and tremendously exciting.

Blind Casting with Lures on the Flats

My guess is that the majority of fishermen approach fishing the flats by blind casting. Faced with a large amount of water, they tie on a lure that they hope will work and start throwing it. When there are a lot of fish around this actually works pretty well. When the water is high or dirty, or the wind is up and/or the sky is overcast you don't have much choice. You can't sight fish effectively under these conditions.

What lure should you use for blind casting? There is no single answer to this, but it ought to be something that you can throw a long way. It also should make noise, or have a lot of flash, or both. If there are a lot of baitfish in the water, more or less imitating them (especially in regards to size) is often a good idea. Surface lures often work well. A weedless spoon likewise is a good choice. I'm not a fan of plugs, but a rattling plug also makes sense if the water is deep enough or grass-free enough to allow its use. A shrimp-tipped bucktail jig, while neither flashy nor noisy, has the scent factor going for it and can also be very effective. What you want to do is let the fish know there is something there that they might be able to eat. You want to attract them to the lure.

Where should you direct your casts? If schools of bait are present, pepper them with casts. Trout, redfish, ladyfish, snook, tarpon, and more all cruise around and under bait schools. Any protruding structure, such as rocks, oysters, stumps, etc. (all rare on Space Coast flats) deserve a few casts. Spoil islands and docks likewise make good targets all through the lagoon system. Drop-offs and sand bars need to be worked. The edges between grass beds and sand holes, and those sand holes themselves, offer good targets. When the water is high enough to allow it, the shoreline itself needs some attention, especially if mangrove trees are growing there.

Don't just pitch your lure mindlessly, and always keep looking to see fish. It doesn't make any sense to allow a good opportunity to slip by because you weren't paying attention.

One other consideration- it pays to have more than one rod rigged when blind casting. Often the lures used for blind casting are flashy and noisy. If you do spot a fish, the sudden increase in noise in his neighborhood that results from a well placed cast may cause him to vacate the premises, pronto. Effective sight casting lures tend to be much more subtle than good blind casting lures. Keep at least one of each rigged up so you're ready for any situation that comes along.

Presentation Off the Beaches

Regardless of the water depth, your offering still has to be in front of the fish if you hope to get a bite. But the situation off the beaches differs tremendously from that on the flats.

Even if you're fishing from the beach, the water is ordinarily fairly deep (by flats stadards) so the fish feel more secure. If you're in a boat frequently the outboard doesn't bother the fish at all (tarpon excepted), and a boat whose motor isn't running seldom bothers them in the least. Speaking generally, ocean fish are harder to spook than are flats fish.

24

Many fish you'll find along or off the beach travel in schools. Spanish mackerel, jack crevalle, tarpon, bluefish, even snook, all tend (when in the ocean) to travel in groups rather than as individuals. Sometimes that school will be tightly packed but often it's more like a large agglomeration of fish. So a cast made anywhere in their general vicinity is likely to bring results.

Sometimes you can see fish in the ocean, making sight fishing possible and effective. Tarpon roll, cobia, tripletail, and barracuda frequently lie underneath floating debris, and a large school of jacks swimming high in the water advertise their presence by actually causing the water color to change (they're visible as a large, darker spot moving through the water). Many times you know fish are there because you can see them busting on the surface as they feed. Spanish mackerel and little tunny frequently clear the water as they pursue bait, making their presence rather obvious. If you see this, don't worry about presentation. Just get your lure there, right now!

So you'll find that most of the time presentation in the sea becomes much less critical than when on the flats. The fish are harder to see, they are generally less spooky, are often more aggressive, and tend to travel in large groups, feeding competitively. If you can find a group of ocean fish, catching them is usually fairly easy.

Chapter 4- About Boats; About Wading

Should I buy a boat? What kind do I need? What is best? Should I fish from the shore? How about that pier over there? Can I catch fish there? Is it safe to wade? Will I see any fish?

As I write this I have 10 boats sitting in my yard (six kayaks, two canoes, a jonboat, and a 17 foot fishing skiff). I own three pairs of flats booties and four pairs of chest waders. I do wade fish quite a bit, and I also fish from several different kinds of boats.

The one kind of fishing I never do is "fish from shore." I see other folks doing this, at bridge crossings, along seawalls, from docks and piers, and along actual shorelines. They are almost always still fishing with bait, something for which I don't have the patience. So I have nothing to say about this topic, other than, if you're interested in shore fishing you probably don't need this book.

boat (bot), n. 1 a hole in the water into which one pours money

The boat. What a piece of equipment it is! Here in Florida many anglers take their boats VERY seriously. It's not at all unusual while on the water here to see state-of-the-art flats skiffs, only 18 feet long, which retail for well over $35,000 for a boat/motor/trailer package.

Undeniably these boats, the Hell's Bay, the Maverick, the Hewes, the Action Craft, and all of the others, are incredibly fine fishing machines which are a joy to own and use. Speaking strictly from the standpoint of the fish, though, for many applications the price of the boat is simply not all that important. Fish don't really care how expensive your boat is! But what features does a good saltwater fishing boat need? What makes it easy to fish from?

Generalizations are difficult due to the wide variety of fishing done here, but any boat used for fishing will need good rod storage to protect expensive rods and reels. A casting area free from protrusions of any type saves many headaches, heartaches, and sometimes broken toes and tackle. For much fishing in the lagoon system a shallow draft, both for running and while actually fishing, is invaluable for getting into skinny areas where redfish, trout, and snook can all be found a great deal of the time. If you spend much time on the pushpole you'll prefer a smaller, lighter vessel.

Boat noise has become one of the most important considerations of all. When there is ripple on the water a noisy boat goes, "bloopbloopbloopbloopbloopbloop...". The fish can hear that noise, and believe me, they have learned what it means. A quiet hull design means you are going to catch more fish in shallow water, and it's worth spending more money to get one.

For anglers who frequently fish along the beaches and out into the ocean a larger and more seaworthy vessel needs serious consideration. Fishermen who prefer to use live bait will need a larger skiff with a good live well that will keep that bait frisky. Once a good fish is hooked, it's important to be able to move around inside the boat without tripping over lots of "stuff." A clean design with adequate storage space is very important. Unfortunately, no one boat handles all chores well, so unless you can afford to own several boats your decision on what to buy will always be a compromise.

For some reason jonboats get little respect. This is a shame since they really are useful in shallow inshore and backcountry areas. You can rig them for fishing very easily and they work extremely well for exploring hazardous areas. My 14 foot MonArk has been dubbed the "Bang-O-Craft" because of its countless scrapes with rocks and oysters. Its tough metal hide absorbs punishment without complaint. It just bounces off and keeps right on motoring along.

Car top boats are not seen as often along the coast as one might expect. Canoes and kayaks make excellent craft for getting back into areas that receive little if any fishing pressure. Serious anglers fishing from canoes carry a pushpole in addition to their paddles. The pole allows both anglers to stand up while searching for fish. The bow man carries the rod while the stern man pushes the boat. After the bow man connects, they trade gear, turn the canoe around, and switch roles. The canoe now goes backwards, the stern man handles the rod, and the bow man poles the boat. It may sound crazy but it works very well for skilled anglers. Give it a try!

Boaters need accessories, too. We will use an anchor as our first example. It needs to hold the boat securely. More importantly, it sometimes needs to be abandoned quickly, especially when a big fish bites. When a big fish strips off line FAST it needs to be chased right now, and pulling the anchor up wastes valuable seconds. Most Florida fishermen use a float on their anchor rope so they can chase fish like this in a hurry. The anchor can be unclipped and left where it is. At the end of the battle the boater returns to retrieve the anchor, or reconnects it to the bow of the boat. Then they continue fishing in exactly the same spot.

Many shallow water anglers use a pushpole for propulsion across the flats. Pushpoles are relatively inexpensive and maintenance free. Some anglers use nothing else.

Electric motors are also very popular. For quiet propulsion in deep water they are vital. You'll see both bow mounts and stern mounts in use. Bow mounts give better control of the boat and have the advantage that you only need one. They work in any depth water too, something that cannot be said of a pushpole. If an electric trolling motor is improperly used it will spook shallow water fish,.

For effective use of stern mounts two (or sometimes even four) are used. Steering is done by the boatman, who uses a pushpole. In other words, the stern mounted electrics assist the poler, rather than replacing him the way the bow mount does. The angler gets the entire front deck to himself, with no one or nothing to get in the way. Some guides use a combination of bow and stern mounts.

Use whatever combination of pushpoles and electrics that suits you best. If the time comes that you need the electrics, you'll know it.

A Primer for Waders

One of the most effective ways to approach game fish, as well as one of the most enjoyable of all the ways to fish, is by getting into the fish's element and wading. The angler has a low profile and keeps the disturbance of the water to a minimum, allowing him to sneak up on feeding fish without spooking them. I have hooked both shallow water redfish and bonefish with literally just the leader out of the fly rod's tip-top. The fish were so close, all I needed to do was dangle the fly in their faces.

For many species of fish, wading will actually be more effective than fishing from a boat. For example, local redfish are heavily pursued by anglers in boats. They have learned that boats are trouble. Getting into casting range from a boat can be tough. A wading angler who keeps quiet can literally get right on top of the fish.

On many days in the winter and spring, strong winds make even the most skilled boat handler want to scream in frustration. Fly fishing in particular is difficult when the boat is moving too fast because of strong winds. Many times it's hard to strip the line fast enough. A wading angler can fish in almost any kind of breeze.

In Space Coast waters during the summer months shorts and some type of protective footwear are all that is needed for comfortable wading. I stepped on a flounder one time while wading barefoot, and although nothing happened as far as injury goes, the incident was all it took to convince me that some sort of shoe really was a good idea. Crabs, oysters, broken bottles, and other hazards to the feet make barefoot wading a stupid thing to do.

The best footwear for wading on flats are neoprene wading boots. These are similar to dive boots, but a stiff plastic sole gives support and protection to the foot. Since they're ankle high, they also keep sand and shells out, and resist the suction effect that soft bottomed areas sometimes dish out. Losing your shoe in bottom ooze in thigh deep water is not fun.

In central Florida, waders make winter wading possible. For those for whom wading is only practiced occasionally, the boot foot type of nylon wader will suffice, although neoprene boots are better. For those for whom wading is a way of life, stocking foot Gore-tex waders are the way to go.

I have had two incidents occur which emphasize the importance of having properly fitting boot foot waders when fishing where the bottom is soft. During an on-the-water seminar one of my students was wearing ill-fitting boot foot waders. As we waded into the water this gentleman took two steps into the water, got stuck in the muck, and fell down. He tried to get back up twice and fell down both times before I could reach him and help him out.

It turned out his boots were two sizes too big. Once he stepped into the mud the boot was mired. When he lifted his foot it came out of the boot. Needless to say he was hog-tied and down he went, unable to even get up again unassisted.

The second incident happened at another seminar, where exactly the same thing happened to another gentleman. If you use boot foot waders make sure they fit well!

Stocking foot waders need wading boots. The area to be fished dictates the type of boot worn. Freshwater trout fishermen will be familiar with felt soled wading boots. These work well where slick, algae covered rocks cover the bottom. On soft muddy bottoms like many of ours, muck sticks to the sole of the felt boots and makes wading practically impossible. In this type of area, the hard soled neoprene wading booties like those mentioned above work much better. You may need to purchase a second pair a size or two larger than your shoe size for use with the neoprene waders.

Waders also need to carry all their paraphernalia. During the winter wading vests are a terrific way to carry tackle and accessories. Many excellent makes are on the market. Make sure the one you buy has enough storage space for everything that you'll need. Remember that metal zippers on pockets will corrode and cease functioning after very little use. Vests with Velcro closures on the pockets are preferred for saltwater fishing.

In the summer vests are usually too hot to be comfortable. One thing to do is carry less stuff. Some fishermen carry extra lures on their hat, others carry accessories in an over the shoulder type of bag. Hip bags are gaining in popularity, and several alternatives to the traditional wading vest have come onto the market in the past few years.

What accessories will you need? This depends on the type of fishing done. Anglers using conventional tackle need extra lures, pliers, and a glove for handling fish as an absolute minimum. Material for making shock leaders, a stringer (see below), water, food, etc. get added to the essentials. You can end up carrying a lot of stuff.

Fly fishermen need more stuff. Although their lures are smaller, they need fly boxes, leader wheels, dry fly floatant, hook files, pliers, clippers, fish glove, and the usual miscellany as described above. Again, it can add up fast if care is not used. Be selective!

Fly fishers may find a stripping basket an absolute essential. Commercially made ones are available, or you can make your own. Rubbermaid laundry baskets make great stripping baskets after you drill the bottom full of holes. An old belt secures it around your waist. If you consistently wade deeply enough that wave action tangles the line in the basket, you can hot glue stick up projections that will keep your line from tangling into the bottom of the basket. These projections are made with string used in weed whackers, available at any garden store.

What techniques can waders use to find fish?

Oftentimes waders can use a boat to find fish, then can anchor up, slip out, and start wading. Two (or more) wading anglers can work a long stretch of shoreline by "leapfrogging", that is, one angler hops out of the boat and starts wading. The other takes the boat downwind (or sun) several hundred yards, then anchors it. He starts wading. When the first angler reaches the boat, he takes it a few hundred yards down from the second angler, anchors it, and so on. If four anglers do this, they can work new water all day long and never have to fish alone. If one is right-handed and the other's a lefty, it works even better.

If while wading down a flat the fish seem scarce, do what guides do and zigzag. Try close to shore and then work farther out. The fish may be on the flat in slightly deeper or shallower water. Look in different depths on the flat and your chances of finding fish improve.

Of necessity much of the angling time spent wading will consist of casting blindly. In general, lures or flies that make noise, especially surface baits like poppers, often work the best for two reasons. First of all, watching and working a popper that you can see is more interesting than retrieving a subsurface lure or streamer that cannot be seen. Secondly, the noise a popper makes attracts fish that might never see an underwater bait. They can hear the popper and come to investigate. And although this is somewhat of an intangible, surface strikes are so much more exciting than underwater ones.

If poppers don't produce, try a flashy lure like a spoon or a rattling plug. Fly fishers might try a streamer fly that pushes water and/or makes noise. Flies with bushy heads like the Seaducer, or flies with bead chain eyes like the Whistler series, or flies with rattles in them, all work well. Some flies have more than one of these features and they can be very effective.

If you're blind casting you want to work as large an area as possible. Fan cast to accomplish this. Cast as far to your left as you can, at say a 90 degree angle to your direction of movement. Then cast at a 60 degree angle, a 30 degree angle, straight ahead, etc., all the way around to 90 degrees to your right. Repeat the process as you move along the flat..

Look for and cast to any areas that you think might hold fish. Cast along oyster beds, rocks, stumps, pilings, drop-offs, the edges of grassy and sandy areas, current edges, eddies, tide rips, schools of bait, or any other area or structure that might hide a fish. In addition to increasing the odds for a strike, your targeting specific locations before every cast will improve your casting skills and this will pay big dividends on future trips.

Always look for signs of fish while wading. Flashes, splashes, tails, wakes, skipping baitfish, swirls- ignore nothing! If fish are seen, try to get into the best possible position from which to cast. Sometimes you have to take any shot you have, but other times the fish are moving slowly and you can get a presentation where the fish is facing you, usually the best kind. The first cast is usually your best opportunity. Try to make it count.

Lastly, use care and common sense when wading, especially in areas with which you are unfamiliar. Make sure the bottom is firm enough to hold you before hopping out of a boat. In all Space Coast waters, stingrays are a cause for caution. Do the "stingray shuffle", never lifting your feet from the bottom. Kicking the ray's wing will cause it to swim away. Pinning it to the bottom will lead to a pierced leg and a trip to the emergency room.

In waters with sharks or alligators (both are found all through the lagoon system), dragging a stringer with fish on it is a huge invitation to trouble. Unless you enjoy going mano a mano with sharks or alligators, this is another good reason to practice catch and release!

If you're fishing from the beach and there is heavy surf, use extreme caution when deciding whether to wade at all. Sure there might be fish out there, but you could easily get knocked down and washed out to sea. The fish will be there another day. Wait until conditions are better.

Finally, although wading can be done as a solo act, safety considerations dictate that you fish with a buddy. So find another fishing maniac and go chase those fish together!

Chapter 5- About Guides; Hazards on the Water; Etiquette; and Respecting the Environment

No, guides are not usually hazards on the water, although there are probably people who think they are. They should be your best friend, but might be your worst nightmare. Good ones are a bargain, bad ones a complete waste of money. Some anglers swear by them, others swear at them. The professional fishing guides that fish the Space Coast are a diverse lot, and like any group of people anywhere hard to make generalizations about.

Anyone considering hiring a guide should ask him some questions before booking the day(s). "What do you charge?" is an obvious start. "What's included?" and "What type of fishing do you do?" are other easy questions. Most guides supply tackle, bait/lures/flies, and license as part of the package. The true professionals will have liability insurance and all necessary permits. Ask before you go.

A question I'm often asked by potential clients is, "What type of boat do you have?" This question is important if three or four people would like to go out on one boat, but as mentioned earlier, fish are generally not impressed by the nameplate on the hull. Although it's true you don't want to fish from a garbage scow there are other, better things to ask about.

During your conversation with the guide, tell him what you want to do. If you will be in the area for several days and need help finding places to fish after your day together, tell him. If you have concerns about your fly casting and would like some instruction, tell him. Honesty now will save misunderstanding and ill will later.

If you can be flexible in your scheduling, ask what days are likely to be most productive. While the guide can't predict the weather or give guarantees, moon phase has a lot to do with fish behavior since it affects tides so much. The guide knows this and also has an experience base from past years. Why book a day that may be unproductive?

If you don't know his reputation ask the guide for references. Often guides develop long term relationships with some of their anglers and fish them the same week every year. Guides with a lot of return business generally entertain and instruct in addition to finding fish. Other guides could find fish in a bathtub but get little if any repeat business because they're obnoxious. If you fish with them you may catch fish, but still hate the entire experience!

Most guides now ask for a deposit to reserve dates, a reasonable request. If an angler changes his mind at the last minute, the guide loses out on a day's wages. Guides get none of the fringe benefits that most salaried workers take for granted. When they're sick or if the weather's bad, they don't get paid. They do not earn retirement pay. While it may look like peaches and cream to the angler, most full time guides work hard for their entire lives and seldom retire anywhere near what most folks would consider financial security. It's a tough way to earn a living, and guides guide because they love it. The financial rewards are few for all but the very best. So don't complain about the deposit, and don't forget to give a good guide a well deserved tip.

The Space Coast is fortunate to have a guides association, the Indian River Guides Association. This organization screens its members, making sure they are licensed and insured and all their legal requirements are met. So if you hire an IRGA member you can be sure that he is operating legally. Their website can be accessed via your computer at www.irga.org.

Hazards and Safety

Hazards? In Florida? Yes, accidents happen everywhere, and Florida isn't immune. Take a look at the hazards you may encounter on any trip along the Space Coast.

Number one has to be insects, primarily mosquitoes, but biting flies and stinging insects can't be forgotten either. Insect repellant and protective clothing takes care of the biters. Controversy increases about the safety of DEET (the active ingredient in most insect repellants), but it definitely does repel insects. It also repels fish and melts down fly lines, so be careful with it.

Some folks like to use Avon's Skin So Soft or other non-DEET repellants. My own experience is that these do not work against anything but no-see-ums. I suspect the individual's attractiveness to and tolerance for bugs determines, in part at least, their effectiveness.

Next comes the sun. Sunburn is an ever present risk in Florida, and skin cancer rates continue rising everywhere. Protect yourself with sunscreen and protective clothing. Dr. William Barnard tells me that he uses the highest SPF sunscreen available whenever he goes fishing regardless of the season, and recommended that I do the same. I pass on his advice to you.

Lightning strikes more people in the state of Florida every year than all other states combined. The majority of those hit are either golfers or anglers. A graphite fishing rod could well be the finest lightning rod ever designed. Is any fish worth a million volt jolt? Find and get under shelter when those threatening thunderheads come rolling your way.

Waders need to concern themselves with three forms of aquatic wildlife. Stingrays are the most prevalent hazard waders face. Seldom aggressive, the rays cover themselves with sand or mud and thus are hard to see. Step on one and it will drive the stinger deep into your leg. The stinger then breaks off while the ray goes about its business, leaving you with an excruciatingly painful souvenir of your encounter. The wound takes months to heal, and everyone I know who has been stung by a ray agrees that it's not an experience you want to have.

Drag your feet while wading. Do the well-known "stingray shuffle." The ray will swim away if you touch the wing. This may startle you, but leaves no lasting mementos.

Alligators swim all through coastal Florida waters. Many folks assume, mistakenly, that gators live only in freshwater. Although gators are seldom aggressive, if you see a big one paying attention to you, get out of the water. Whatever you do, don't drag fish on a stringer while gators are around!

Gators often rest on the bottom in shallow water, so be careful when you wade. I seldom see gators in Space Coast waters during the winter months. We never worry about them then. During the warmer months we watch much more closely and in waters where there are lots of them we are much more hesitant about getting out of the boat.

Sharks present almost no danger, unless you are dragging a stringer of fish. However, they certainly deserve respect, especially when the surf gets full of big ones. The mullet run will bring large sharks in close to shore. Consider fishing from the beach then!

Other boaters possibly present the greatest hazard of all. Florida has the highest boating fatality rate in the nation. Alcohol is often a contributing factor in boating accidents. Stay sober and consider wearing a life vest when traveling from spot to spot.

A well prepared angler knows the hazards and acts accordingly. In addition, common sense dictates always carrying a first aid kit. All anglers, all <u>adults</u> need to know basic first aid techniques. Although you hope you never need them, you never know when you will. Take a standard first aid course at your first opportunity.

Etiquette on the Water

It should not come as surprise that there are more and more boats on the water all the time. Thanks to displaced Yankees like me, Spanish speaking peoples from all over the Americas, and many other peoples from many other countries, all of whom are looking for Paradise, central Florida is growing at an astounding rate. Apparently the developers won't be satisfied until every last square inch of the state is paved over.

Unfortunately, lots of boats around seldom enhances the angling experience. You have heard of road rage. Sadly, there are cases of river rage, too.

What usually happens in these cases is one party gets upset at a perceived infringement upon what they are doing by a second party. The second party is usually guilty of one of the following circumstances:

1) Ignorance. They know so little about shallow water fishing that they don't realize they are getting in the way or ruining your fishing.

2) Circumstance. Especially on weekends, there are sometimes so many boats out that no matter which way you go you can't help but get in someone's way. There's not much you can do about this but fish in less popular spots.

3) It could be that they're just a jerk. Obviously, if you're reading this you're not! Fortunately, no more than about five percent of the folks out there fit in this category. These people just don't care if they piss you off. But when there are a lot of boats out there you are bound to run into some of them.

Fishing is supposed to be enjoyable, but when guys are yelling and cursing at each other from boat to boat it's not. So here are a few guidelines that, if followed, will keep confrontations to a minimum.

<u>At the Ramp-</u>

-Stage your boat before you back onto the ramp. Keep your time on the ramp to a minimum.

-If it's dark, shut off your headlights when backing. If your lights are on no one else can see where they're going because you're blinding them.

-Once your boat is off the trailer, clear it and your vehicle from the ramp as quickly as possible.

-When loading your boat onto the trailer after fishing, again, keep your actual ramp time to a minimum. Clear the ramp and get out of the way before prepping your boat for the road. Remember, other people are waiting for you!

On the Water-
-Do not run your motor when you're near other boats that are fishing. This is especially true in shallow water. If you can see what color the other boat is you're probably too close.
-Do not run the flats to find fish, especially on weekends. Once you burn a flat it's ruined for hours, maybe for the rest of the day.
-Find your own fish. Yes, those guys over there are hooked up. That doesn't mean they want you there. Would you like it if they moved in on you?

Sometimes you'll see two, three, even four boats working a school of fish together. Almost without exception, the people in these boats know each other. If you move in, you will probably not be made to feel welcome.

Now it is a credible argument to say, "Well, they don't own those fish." That is undeniably true. However, I repeat the question- Would you like it if they moved in on you if it were you on some fish?

Yelling at other fishermen does nothing but make a bad situation worse. Try not to let testosterone get in the way of good judgment.

Please keep it in your mind that a lot of friction would be eliminated if we all treated our neighbors the way we would like to be treated. Wouldn't it be wonderful if we all followed the rule, "Do unto others as you would have them do unto you"?

Respect for the Environment

Mother Earth supports our existence. She created the habitat where we live and where we all fish. We live on a most wonderful planet, yet the lack of respect that we humans show for our natural world continually shocks, angers, and saddens me.

As an individual angler there's not much you can do about human population growth, deforestation, desertification, suburban sprawl, etc., etc., ad nauseum. But there are plenty of smaller ways to make a difference:

-Treat your catch with respect. If you're going to eat your catch, kill it humanely. A three foot length of 2 x 2 applied smartly to the back of the head will dispatch most fish quickly. For oily fish like mackerel or bluefish, gut and bleed them immediately. Regardless of the species, put fish destined for the table on ice right away.

Fish to be released should be kept in the water as much as possible and handled as little as possible. To release a gut-hooked fish, cut the line as close to the mouth as possible.

How you revive a fish depends on the species. Fish like jacks, mackerel, and little tunny should be "torpedoed," that is, launched into the water head first. If they are held out of the water very long they will not recover.

Redfish, seatrout, tarpon, and snook need to be held by the jaw and tail and gently

34

moved back and forth in the water until they can swim off strongly. If released over a seagrass bed, redfish and trout frequently get tangled in the grass. Since they're already tired from being caught, they usually roll over and die when this happens. Try to release them over sand spots.

-Know where you're going. A casual examination of almost any grass flat in Florida will show that a lot of boaters don't follow this rule. Grass beds support the food chain that the game fish depend on. Prop scarring of grass beds just keeps getting worse. Many times prop scarring happens when boaters suddenly find themselves in water much shallower than they had expected.

-Do not run the flats. Although I suspect most fishermen use this technique on occasion, running the flats is an exercise for the lazy or unskilled. It disrupts the fishing and the fish. It is practiced so much in the Mosquito Lagoon that the behavior of the fish is changing to avoid the constant engine noise through the shallow water environment. Lastly, it damages the grass beds, and thus the fishing.

-Dispose of you trash properly. It's probably OK to toss an apple core or a banana peel into the water. Cans, bottles, plastic bags, soft plastic fishing lures, and particularly fishing lines never belong in the water.

Think about it. You break off fish. You get hung up and break your line. Paper and plastic blow out of the boat. Soft plastics tear off while fighting fish. Outboard motor operation adds pollutants to both air and water. We're littering all the time no matter how conscientious we are. There's no sense adding to it intentionally because we're lazy or careless.

I make it a point to pick up other people's trash whenever I can, trying to make up for what litter I inadvertently cause. If we all did this our environment would be the better for it.

One Last Thought...

Recreational fishing is under attack by misinformed people and groups such as PETA. Clean up after yourself and others, and try to behave in a responsible manner. It's up to no one but ourselves to keep our image as stewards of the environment untarnished

Chapter 6- Fly Fishing Along the Space Coast

Plenty of fly fishing opportunities for some very exciting and sometimes quite large fish await the adventurous fly fisher here. Redfish, seatrout, tarpon, snook, crevalle, and ladyfish are all common catches in the lagoon system. Along the beaches you can catch these same fishes, as well as Spanish mackerel, cobia, tripletail, bluefish, little tunny, and more.

The Basic Outfit

For day-in, day-out fishing for redfish, snook, and seatrout use an eight-weight outfit with a rod that's nine feet long. This rod has plenty of power to push large flies into the wind, be they streamers or surface baits like poppers or hair bugs. It's got the strength to double-haul a large fly into the wind, or stop a tarpon up to fifty pounds (or larger, in skilled hands). Persons fishing mostly for smaller fish, or skilled anglers, may prefer a seven or even a six-weight.

Most fly fishers will be best advised to bring a floating weight-forward line. Especially for fishing the lagoon system, I strongly recommend over-lining your rod by at least one line weight. In lagoon fishing accuracy and speed of delivery are critical components to catching fish. If you can cast 50 feet accurately and get the fly to the target immediately you will catch your share of fish. If you have to make eight or ten false casts to make a 40 foot cast you need lessons and practice.

Intermediates, sinktips, full sinkers, shooting heads, etc. can be used as necessity dictates. These lines will be of more use in the Atlantic than in the lagoons. A sinking line is helpful when casting in the surf, but it's a hindrance when the water is only 18 inches deep.

Make sure the reel is as full as possible. This is done by adding backing underneath the fly line. For saltwater fish, backing is important for fighting the fish. A fly line is only about one hundred feet long, and most sizeable saltwater fish will pull that much line off in just a few seconds. The backing, usually 20 pound test Dacron for an eight- or a nine-weight, is attached to the rear of the fly line so the fish can continue its run without coming up abruptly against the end of the fly line. You need at least 100 yards of backing, and you'll likely need more if you'll be fishing in the ocean.

If you'll be fishing in the ocean for tarpon, big crevalle, sharks, or other really big fish you'll need a heavier outfit. Hundred pound plus tarpon pretty much demand a 12-weight. Scale your tackle to the size of the fish anticipated.

Leaders

For most saltwater applications I prefer the big game type of leader. For smaller fish it's not needed, but you can run into fish over 20 pounds anywhere in Space Coast waters at almost any time. I prefer to be prepared for those kinds of encounters.

Whip a loop in the end of the fly line. Attach a five-to-six foot butt section of 30 pound test to the end of the fly line by looping the leader butt to it. Tie a loop in the other end of the butt. When attaching the rest of the leader, simply make a loop-to-loop connection between the leader and the butt. This makes changing leaders fast and simple- no knots to tie.

To make a tippet section take a six foot (more or less) section of 15 pound fluorocarbon leader material and tie a Bimini twist in one end. Then tie a double surgeon's loop in the doubled line, and loop this to the leader butt. If no shock tippet is needed just tie the fly to the point.

As mentioned earlier in this work, many saltwater fish have sharp or abrasive teeth. For this reason, shock leaders are attached between the end of the leader and the fly. The shock is usually eight to twelve inches long, and can be as light as 20 pound fluorocarbon or as heavy as 80 or 100 pound, depending on what kind of fish you hope to catch. The chart on leaders found on p. 42 will be of use to fly casters, too.

Knots

Anyone getting involved in saltwater fly fishing should learn these knots- the Albright special, for attaching wire bite tippet to the leader; the Bimini twist, for tying up leaders; the Uni-knot (also called the Duncan loop) for attaching flies to the shock leader; the double surgeons knot, for tying loops in leaders for the loop-to-loop system and also for tying leader sections together. You really should know how to whip a loop in the end of the fly line, too.

An excellent book that shows how to tie these knots is Practical Fishing Knots by Mark Sosin and Lefty Kreh. This book, combined with some leader material and a few hours practice, will make most folks competent knot tiers of which even the Boy Scouts could be proud.

Flies

Lure selection, whether for fly or conventional tackle, is a very personal thing, based on a combination of knowledge, intuition, and past experience. A glimpse at Lefty Kreh's book, "Salt Water Fly Patterns", reveals that literally thousands of fly patterns have been devised, all with the same purpose- to entice a fish into striking.

Do all these flies work? Most definitely. Does the salt water fly fisherman need a barge to carry his fly boxes? Most definitely not.

When wading I usually only have room for one fly box. Only a few fly patterns will fit, so I choose those flies which have proven themselves to me, ones which I have confidence in and which I know meet my needs.

Where you live and what you fish for most of the time will color your choice of flies, of course. In spite of this, some flies are so universal in their appeal to gamefish of all types that they need to be carried by almost all saltwater fly rodders. Certainly in my own travels along the coast from Maine to Louisiana I see the same classic patterns in the fly boxes of all the excellent fly fishers that it's been my good fortune to meet.

Lefty's Deceiver is a superb example of this universal type of fly. With its shape imitating that of so many different types of baitfish, its ability to be adapted and modified to fit differing conditions, and because it can be tied in sizes ranging from two inches to over ten inches in length, Deceivers can be and are used to catch everything from panfish to billfish. All fly fishers need to carry a selection of these flies in various sizes and colors. At the small end a #4 Deceiver will imitate smaller sized baitfish very well. For fishing for big fish off the beaches a 3/0 hook in a fly with a six inch length often isn't big enough. Deceivers can be tied with a wide variety of natural and synthetic materials, in both weighted and unweighted versions.

Last year while painstakingly trying to match feathers for Deceivers a light bulb went off in my head. "Why not just tie Blondes?" it said. In most situations Blondes work just as well as Deceivers and are a heck of a lot easier to tie.

Bob Clouser's Deep Minnow is another example of a fly that all game fish will eat. A simple tie of lead, steel, and bucktail, more than fifty different species of fish have been taken on Clouser minnows. They are a standard on everything from striped bass to bonefish. Carry these flies in sizes 4, 2, and 1, with various sized lead eyes so you can adapt to different situations. Favorite color combinations include chartreuse and white and tan and white. Remember to keep these flies sparse, use some flash, and be sure to have some with weedguards.

Poppers of one sort or another add so much enjoyment to the fly fisher's life. What in all fishing can be more exciting than seeing a big fish come to the surface and attack a fake minnow at the end of your line? Although size is important in surface flies, colors seems much less so. You should have smaller sized poppers and some which you think would scare the fish to death. Whether you choose deerhair, cork, or the newer plastic foam poppers is a matter of personal choice. Keep in mind a bluefish will chew a hair bug to nothing in no time. Plastic may lack aesthetics, but it sure is durable!

Diving flies have become justly popular in recent years. Larry Dahlberg developed the first diving bug, using deerhair to make the head. Foam divers are available now. Regardless of the material they're made from, divers are effective on a wide variety of fish.

A variety of different crab flies have been developed. The first ones, for example, the McCrab, were tied from deerhair and were unwieldy things to cast. In spite of these shortcomings, fish ate them. Now crab imitations are tied from many different materials, and their use is spreading from southern waters up the Atlantic coastline, from being used exclusively for permit and bonefish to red and black drum, weakfish, and even stripers. Stripers like crabs! My own favorite crab pattern is a yarn crab called a Merkin.

The Homer Rhodes shrimp fly, now commonly called the Seaducer, is another saltwater classic useful everywhere. Rhodes designed the fly to take bonefish in the Florida Keys. One past summer I found that stripers in New Hampshire and Massachusetts liked this pattern a lot! Lots of different fish will take this fly and it should also be carried in a variety of sizes and colors. Seaducers can also be weighted with lead eyes, which gives them an undulating action many fish find irresistible.

For fishing in areas that are shallow and have grassy bottoms, or oysters, or rocks, or anything else that could catch the point of a conventionally tied fly, reverse-tied flies like bendbacks are a necessity. Anywhere snag-filled shallows hold fish that eat flies a bendback fly is a good choice.

For fishing in deeper waters, especially those with currents, Blanton's Whistler proved its worth a long time ago. Designed to produce vibrations and work like a jig, it's especially effective in discolored water. Again, this fly takes a wide variety of species.

Some of the more recent developments in the world of saltwater flies have near-universal applications, too. Bob Popovics' Siliclone jumps to mind. While these flies are hard to cast they are invaluable when the fish are feeding on mullet.

SexyFlies are flies that need to be carried by anyone fishing the Atlantic waters along the Space Coast. These are superb tarpon flies, and will take many other species of fish as well. Although these flies can be tied up to be quite bulky, the synthetic materials from which they're made shed water easily. They're easy to cast. You can trim them to any shape you want. My favorite is a pilchard shape, especially useful when chumming with these gamefish-attracting baits. These flies are very durable, too.

So we have listed here ten different patterns which will cover the entire water column from the surface to the inky depths and which will take almost any species of saltwater gamefish found anywhere. There's no need to carry a hundred different fly patterns!

Anglers who specialize in certain niches may well need to carry other patterns. Although it is not the intention of this book to cover all of the endless possibilities, we can devote some space to the more obvious ones. Anglers fishing for mackerel or bluefish need flies that will hold up to the onslaught of viselike jaws and piranha-like teeth. Bob Popovics' Surf Candy series, with their epoxy bodies and synthetic materials, resist the worst blues can dish out. A few winter days spent at the tying vise can result in an entire season's supply of Candy.

Barracuda are an excellent fly rod target, but have unusual dietary preferences. Long streamers tied to imitate needlefish are among the most effective barracuda flies. Although these are definitely one fish-one fly ties, fortunately they're easy to make.

Tarpon. Many anglers believe it is the ultimate fly rod fish. I'm inclined to agree. Stu Apte developed what turned out to be the classic tarpon streamer for fishing on flats. Although tied with many different color combinations, and while other materials are now being used besides the basic hackle feathers, Apte's original design is still the standard tie for tarpon flies. It's fairly easy to tie, it resists fouling, it casts well, and tarpon eat it. What more could a fisherman want in a fly?

Every fly fisher, especially if he ties his own flies, will favor certain patterns. He'll modify patterns to suit his needs. If he's observant, clever, and innovative, he'll develop new patterns to fill a need others haven't seen. His fly box will hold a combination of those classic standards that work anywhere and those special flies that work well in his own unique situation.

Use the patterns described here to begin to stock your own box, and use your own experiences to try to finish the job. You'll find, as all other fly fishers before you have, that this job never stops. New materials, new ideas, new patterns, continually pour out from the fertile minds of great fly fishers everywhere.

Please let me know about your own innovations and successes!

Top Ten List of Effective Saltwater Fly Patterns

1) Clouser Deep Minnow, chartreuse and white, tan and white, black, and various other color combinations, sizes 4, 2, 1 (in various weights, and some with weedguards).

2) Lefty's Deceiver/Brooks Blonde, color to match local baitfish, sizes 4 through 3/0.

3) Seaducer (Homer Rhodes Shrimp Fly), some weighted, red and yellow, yellow and grizzly, red and white, plain grizzly, size 2 to 2/0 (some with weedguards).

4) Merkin crab, tan and brown, size 2 (some with weedguards).

5) Popping bugs, size 2 to 2/0 (some with weedguards).

6) Bendbacks, size 2, 1, colored to imitate local shrimp, crabs, or baitfish.

7) Whistlers, size 1 to 3/0. This is typically an attractor pattern, so try bright color combinations like red and white or red and yellow.

8) Siliclones, size 2 to 2/0. Color to match local bait. In Florida gray and grizzly works well.

9) Divers, either Dahlberg style or foam, size 2 to 1/0 (some with weedguards).

10) SexyFlies, tied to match local bait fish in size and color (some with weedguards).

Chapter 7- Nearshore How To

The Space Coast offers fabulous nearshore fishing to the small boat angler with some savvy. "Nearshore" for our purposes means from the beach out to a distance of perhaps six or seven miles. If you're nearshore by my definition, then you can plainly see the shoreline.

For the small boat angler nearshore fishing is a three season sport. In the winter the Atlantic is just too rough most of the time for small boats. Fishing loses some of its fascination when passengers are vomiting and you can't stand up without falling out of the boat. However, on those bluebird winter days when the seas lie down some good fishing can be had.

The ocean can get rough in any season, so pick your days carefully, and always watch for changes in the weather. The only advantage that sinking during the summer has over sinking in the winter is that hypothermia is less likely when the water temperature is in the 80's.

Always carry all of the USCG required gear. A VHF radio and a cell phone are both good items to have with you in case you get into trouble. A GPS unit will pinpoint your position in case someone has to come looking for you. Two or even three boats working together is always a good, safe way to prowl the nearshore waters.

Electronics other than a GPS that can come in handy in the search for fish include a quality depth recorder and a thermometer that will display the water temperature. Since I have neither of these I sometimes don't do as well out there as I otherwise might. Monitoring the VHF radio can lead to tidbits of usable information that could lead to a big payoff, too.

Ocean access on the Space Coast comes from three locations: Ponce de Leon Inlet to the north, Port Canaveral in the central Space Coast area, and Sebastian Inlet to the south. By far the safest of the three is the Port. Locks inside the Port keep water from the Banana River Lagoon from running out of the Port, so standing waves are almost never a problem at the Port entrance. At the other two inlets a strong outgoing tide combined with an east wind (an almost daily occurrence during the summer months) make for large standing waves and frequently very dangerous navigation through the jetties.

Nearshore Tackle and Rigging

Fish encountered while fishing nearshore run from snapper bluefish of a pound or two to Spanish mackerel to giant crevalle to king mackerel to large tarpon to larger sharks. Clearly, the well prepared angler will carry an assortment of high quality, well maintained tackle, because when you're on the ocean you just never know what will take your bait.

Ten pound spinning or plug outfits are a great deal of fun, and perfectly adequate for bluefish, ladyfish, smaller jacks, Spanish mackerel, slot sized reds, beach snook, tripletail under debris, barracuda, etc. When you start looking for big tripletail under moored structure, cobia, big kings, big jacks, big tarpon, or sharks, a 20 or even a 30 pound spinning or conventional outfit is a much more practical tool. Anyone who's caught a 30 pound crevalle on any kind of tackle can testify that a wimpy rod (or attitude!) is not what's needed in that situation. Don't go out looking for big fish when you're undergunned.

Regardless of the size of your outfit you'll need a leader. The lightest one that will work for whatever you hope to catch is what you should use. Usually you'll garner more strikes using fluorocarbon, rather than monofilament, leaders.

Fish	Suggested Leader
snapper blues*, redfish, small jacks, ladyfish, Spanish mackerel*, tripletail under debris, snook	about 3 feet of 30 pound fluorocarbon *expect some cutoffs
Cobia, big jacks, big tripletail under structure	3 to 5 feet of 50 pound fluorocarbon
big tarpon	80 to 100 pound fluorocarbon, as long as you can comfortably throw.
king mackerel, barracuda, sharks	18 to 24 inches of single strand wire

Nearshore Strategies

Author's Note: Since 9/11/01, all nearshore waters north of Port Canaveral up to Playalinda Beach for a distance of three miles out from the beach have been closed to all civilian vessels. The fine is up to $50,000 and up to five years in prison. The US Coast Guard station at Port Canaveral has more information. Contact them at 321.853.7601.

The best way to keep track of the fish is to go fishing every day, or have a close friend who does AND who doesn't mind sharing information. In the ocean a day or two can make a big difference in the location of the fish.

Barring the above, what do you look for when heading out into the Atlantic? Time of year makes a big difference in your approach, so let's start there.

During the spring months the two main species of fish that nearshore anglers hunt are cobia and tripletail, although bluefish and Spanish mackerel may also be available. When I launch my boat (almost always at Port Canaveral) the first sign I'm looking for is clean water, very closely followed by floating sargassum weed. Always be on the lookout for other flotsam of any kind. If you find any check it carefully for fish.

Once you leave the jetties at the Port a line of buoys runs out almost four miles towards the southeast, marking the main shipping channel into the port. Both tripletail and cobia relate to these buoys, so that's a good place to start. However, every fisherman coming out of the port knows that too, so unless you're an early riser someone will have already been there.

If you can find a line of weeds simply idle along and follow it. Sooner or later you will find some fish. Tripletail love to relate to flotsam of any kind and a big weed mat will usually have some tripletail under it. Bait presentation for tripletail you can see is different than for most other fish. Either cast past the fish and bring the bait to him, or try to drop it right on his noggin if it's a softer type of bait. Although tripletail will take a wide variety of baits and lures, it's hard to beat a jumbo live shrimp.

Cobia also like flotsam, and frequently swim along weedlines searching for small fish and crabs. They will eat anything a tripletail will, and similarly, a live jumbo shrimp is hard for them to refuse. Dollar-sized blue crabs are another excellent, if hard to find, cobia bait. Cobia are quite fond of small eels. Personally, I think I'll just stick with the jumbo shrimp.

Cobia can also be found by any buoys you may encounter. But the favorite technique for cobia during the spring months, at least out of the Port, is to find a free swimming manta ray. The rays will usually be two to four miles offshore and generally heading north. They often have a flock of cobia with them.

Although I've had good success with the DOA BaitBuster, most anglers who do this type of fishing use a large (two to four ounce) chartreuse jig, known locally as a "cobia jig." The jig is cast ahead of and past the ray, and worked so that it passes right over (or under) it. Be careful not to foul hook the ray!

If a cobia shows interest in your lure but doesn't take, speed up the retrieve. Sometimes, like jacks, they just don't get excited by a lure that's too easy to catch. Make it look like it's trying to escape and they frequently jump all over it.

The manta rays usually come by the Port Canaveral area during March and April. Although you may find a straggler anytime, by the end of April the nearshore cobia fishing is nearly done.

Another fish that shows up off the port this time of year are the oceanic jack crevalle. Although they sometimes come in close to the beach, they are usually found out from two to five miles. These fish run between 20 and 40 pounds and will destroy your tackle when they're eating well. With nice weather schools of hundreds of them will swim at the surface in 40 or 50 feet of water. While they will of course take lures or flies (poppers work particularly well), when they're being fussy (yes, they sometimes are) a small live fish of almost any kind will work. Pinfish and mullet are personal favorites, as are pogies when they show up.

When the water temperatures rise into the 70's, the menhaden (also called pogies or bunker) schools start showing up. King mackerel love them, and the kings show up at about the same time. Most king fishermen out of the port will net up sufficient number of pogies for a day's fishing (you'll need a good livewell system, as pogies die easily) and then slow troll them (idle speed) on kingfish stinger rigs.

Different fishermen make these rigs different ways, but the basic system is a 12 to 15 inch long piece of number three (30 to 40 pound test) single strand wire. At one end is a black barrel swivel and at the other is a size 1/0 to 3/0 bronze bait hook (some guys use trebles).

Wired to the eye of the bait hook is another piece of wire four or five inches long. To this a size 1 or 2 bronze treble hook is haywire twisted. To use the rig, the pogy is hooked through the nose with the lead hook, and hooked in the back with the trailer, or stinger.

Kings like to clip the bait in half, swallowing the tail and often leaving the head. With this rig you still hook those short strikers.

The nearshore kings are frequently found around the buoy line, sometimes right at the port entrance when the bait is thick. South of there they could be anywhere, but are frequently two or more miles out from the beach. There are some excellent kingfish spots farther out (Pelican Flats and the 8A Reef), but that's beyond the scope of this book.

Kent Gibbens told me there's excellent king fishing out of Ponce Inlet during the summer. He says a lot of anglers there troll large lipped plugs such as the Bomber so they don't have to mess with the pogies. Kent's own personal favorite lure for this is the Redfin, a much smaller plug. He also said an effective and fairly effortless way to catch kings out of Ponce Inlet is to get some jumbo live shrimp and then liveline them on an outgoing tide at the color line where the inlet water and ocean water meet.

Terry Parsons likewise says excellent king mackerel fishing can be had out of Sebastian Inlet. The gig is largely the same as has been described above. Terry says he always catches the biggest fish near the beach, in less than 20 feet of water.

Tarpon require 75 degree or warmer water. They show up in early summer as soon as the water temperature is high enough. Beach tarpon along the Space Coast are usually big ones, averaging 100 pounds or so. They, like the king mackerel, love to eat pogies and are frequently found around pogy pods, regardless of what depth the water might be. Consequently, tarpon could be right in the surf or out several miles from the beach. Anglers slow trolling pogies for king mackerel frequently hook tarpon, as well as those big jacks and quite a few sharks, too.

If you want to target tarpon a good strategy is to net up some pogies (or mullet) and cruise along the beach, just beyond the breakers. Look for bait pods that have pelicans working them. As soon as you see this shut down and watch for rolling or busting fish. An electric trolling motor is almost a necessity for this fishing. When you see fish, try to determine if the fish are moving or not. If they are, move to a location where you can shut down and let them swim to you. You will be quieter and have better success if you do this.

If they are more or less stationary use the electric motor to quietly move near enough to liveline a pogy, using the electric motor to maintain the same general position. If you don't have a trolling motor, set up a wind drift so you can approach the area without spooking the fish, and then anchor up. Again, liveline your bait into the area where the fish were observed.

Sometimes when the water surface glasses out the tarpon will lay up at the surface. I've seen big schools of them like this several miles offshore. It's a great chance to fly fish them, but only if you have a trolling motor. There is no other way to approach them.

The king mackerel and tarpon fishing described above is available all summer long. But what every angler who owns a boat and lives within driving distance of the Space Coast eagerly awaits every year is the end of August and the start of...

...The Mullet Run

Florida east coast mullet come in two varieties. The black, or striped, mullet is a robust fish that can grow to 15 pounds if it manages to live long enough, although the average size is around 12 inches. The silver ("finger") mullet is a much smaller fish, averaging four to six inches in length and topping off at about one foot. Black mullet spawn in south Florida waters, at the edge of the Gulf Stream, by which they disperse their eggs. Silver mullet are tropical in nature, so when the water temperature starts to drop, usually some time in September, they start heading south.

At the peak of the run millions and millions of finger mullet swim south along the beach, turning the water black, looking like a fluid, living river at the edge of the sea. Fountains of small fish erupt from the water, chased by predators from below. Tarpon, kingfish, and Spanish mackerel free-jump through the baitfish as they gorge themselves, and schools of ravenous jack crevalle rip through the helpless bait. Pelicans, terns, and gulls, hovering and screaming, wait for their chance to intercept their share of the silvery tidbits of protein swimming below.

Life is not easy for a mullet. Fortunately a female mullet produces millions of eggs, because on their southwards migration mullet are eaten by the millions by every predator in the sea. Tarpon, snook, redfish, Spanish mackerel, king mackerel, jack crevalle, various species of sharks, barracuda, ladyfish, seatrout and especially bluefish, all these and more eat huge numbers of migrating mullet.

I usually fish two lines, live-lining a mullet on one. On this one the catch is typically bluefish, Spanish mackerel, and ladyfish. Another line will carry a mullet weighed down with a one ounce egg sinker. Fish such as snook and redfish usually come on the sinker rig. Tarpon, crevalle, and sharks will take either depending on where in the water column they happen to be.

Capt. Eric Davis runs the beaches near the Sebastian Inlet, preferring to fish for tarpon, but taking his share of snook, jacks, and other species. "I run the beach and concentrate on finding schools of bait that have birds working over them. Pelicans or terns are the best. I usually find tarpon working schools of bait where pelicans are diving. I prefer fishing using fly tackle, with my favorite fly being the PolarFiber Minnow. But when that doesn't work I'll live bait them with freshly cast-netted mullet."

Eric says the fish seem to come in waves. "Fishing will be really good for a few days, then it will slow down for a week, then pick up again. It's not a steady movement of fish down the beach. You have to go out there and run the beach and look, and some days you won't find much. But other days it will be incredible, and you'll be in big fish until you are too worn out to fish any more.

Even if you can't reach the mullet because of the weather, it's still worth going to the beach just to watch. Big tarpon free jump through schools of bait, and sharks explode into schools of mullet that are running for their lives. It is definitely worth the price of admission."

As the mullet peter out (usually sometime in November) the snook, tarpon, kingfish, big jacks, and cudas follow them south and are gone. While the mullet still run though, northeast breezes will begin concentrating lines of sargassum weed out off the beaches a few miles.

Tripletail and cobia once again become a favored target until the Atlantic gets too rough to go out on anymore, usually around Thanksgiving.

Also, once the mullet finish passing (around the end of October), there are still big schools of glass minnows (bay anchovies, or silversides) coming down the beach. These minnows are a favored forage of the Spanish mackerel, who follow them south.

The mackerel are big, fat, end of summer fish, frequently averaging four to five pounds and sometimes even more. They get incredibly thick. On a good day you can literally be in boiling, free jumping mackerel for as far as you can see. With light spinning or fly tackle you can catch fish until you are tired of it. Sometimes it really does get too easy. Rarely, little tunny will be in there with them, so don't get too complacent.

Glass minnows are small baits, so your lure should be small too. My own favorites are small streamer flies or popping bugs, delivered on a five- or six-weight fly outfit. For spin fishers, a small silver spoon, small white jig, or a small, white, soft plastic minnow imitation (like the CAL shad from DOA lures) all work well. A 30 pound fluorocarbon leader will guarantee plenty of bites but you will also lose a lot of lures, so have plenty with you.

This fishing also lasts well into November. Then cold fronts start coming through, the ocean gets riled up, and until the following spring it's generally too rough to go out any more. Then the nearshore Space Coast fisherman stays inshore- until Spring arrives.

Chapter 8- When To Fish

One question which almost every angler who comes across the bow of my skiff asks is, "When is fishing the best here?" Since the question defies a simple answer, I don't like it.

As an example of how perplexing answering this question can be, I cite the following experience. An excellent fly caster by the name of Rusty Chinnis hired me for two days in March a few years back. I knew where there was a school of jumbo reds, and the first morning I took him straight there. Inside of five minutes Rusty was hooked up to a fish that turned out to measure a whopping 28 pounds on the Boga Grip.

In the process of fighting this fish we spooked the rest of the school and we couldn't find them again, so we went to another spot where I thought there would be a number of smaller fish. Never for a moment did I dream what would greet us there.

Rusty and I went wading. There were hundreds of fish, so thick they were literally bumping into my legs. Fly fishing, I got three fish with only a foot of leader out of the tip of the rod, just dangling the fly in the fish's faces. Between us we probably got 50 fish to 13 pounds. It was the best day of redfishing I ever expect to experience.

The next morning we went back to the school of big fish. They wouldn't let us near them with the skiff, so we tried wading to them. After an hour Rusty had had only one cast at them, which spooked them. He finally said, "Let's go to that other place," which we did.

We staked out the skiff and went wading again. After an hour we had seen exactly one redfish, where the day before there had been hundreds. Rusty said, "I can't take this after yesterday. I want to go home." He was serious, so we were back at the dock by about 10:30 AM.

Back to back days, the same spots, the same angler, slightly different weather, vastly different results. In the lagoon system on any given day you could have the day of a lifetime, or get utterly and completely skunked. I can't predict it.

So, the best time to go fishing is whenever you can, and the best time to catch fish is when they're biting. The biggest truism in fishing is that if you're not out there, you definitely will not catch anything.

That having been said, there can be no denying that the fishery, both in the lagoon system and in the ocean, changes with the seasons. So, let us examine how the fishing changes through the year with a discussion of the seasons.

Winter

Winter in these parts, as defined by temperature rather than date, starts around Thanksgiving and runs until around mid-March. This is subjective and changes from year to year. Water temperatures during this time of year are usually in the 60's, although during a cold stretch they could drop into the 50's, or in a warm spell inch into the 70's. Similarly, average daytime air temperatures usually start in the 50's and rise into the high 60's or low 70's, but could be below freezing or into the 80's. Since the weatherman can't predict the weather with anything more than about 50 percent accuracy, don't expect anything better from me!

Since the water temperatures are too low for many species, depending on where you are the main species of fish you'll run into in the lagoon system this time of year are our three year-round residents: seatrout, redfish, and black drum. Other species encountered include ladyfish, flounder, sheepshead, and bluefish, and possibly crevalle around the Sebastian Inlet.

The major weather feature at this time of year is the cold front. The fronts come in from the west or northwest, always bring wind, often bring rain, and are always followed by lower temperatures, low humidity, high pressure, and usually clear blue skies. The day after the front passes it's frequently windy out of the northwest, and as subsequent days pass the air warms, the humidity rises, and the wind shifts around to the north, northeast, east, and finally southeast. Then eventually another front comes through, and the pattern repeats.

When this pattern repeats on a weekly basis it can lead to very predictable and usually excellent fishing. The falling water temperatures and rapid change in atmospheric pressure immediately following the passage of the front pushes almost all fish off the flat. Where do they go? That depends on the degree of the temperature change.

If the front is fairly weak they'll get into nearby deeper water. If it's a strong front with a large drop in temperature the fish will be forced to find thermal refuges in deep water locations such as dredge holes and canals. Water temperatures that drop too fast during the wintertime frequently lead to fish kills.

As soon as the wind settles and the temperature begins to moderate the fish will be back up on the flat, often times first thing in the morning. Both seatrout and redfish seem to enjoy sunning themselves in potholes in the grass in very shallow water at this time of year. Although not feeding aggressively, they will definitely take a well-placed bait.

Another behavior that you may observe during the winter is that redfish, and to a lesser degree seatrout, will often school up, especially during the warm-up immediately following very cold weather. This is the only time of year I ever see big groups of trout all sunning themselves in shallow water. Sight fishing for seatrout can be excellent during the winter, in my experience the only time of year that this is true.

When I go fishing on my own at this time of year I often see folks pulling out their boats as I'm arriving. They are frequently complaining about how bad the fishing was. Now, think about this. The water is cold. The nights are long, and at night radiational cooling allows the water to cool off even more. Fish are cold blooded creatures. They are going to be most active during the warmest part of the day during the winter, and unless the air is not moving at all this won't be until the afternoon, frequently not until sunset. Dawn patrol starts are not necessary during the winter months, and most of the time will be counterproductive.

If the wind is blowing and the sun is out, try to find lee shorelines with a southern exposure. Deep water access nearby is frequently a plus. Fish will often be sunning themselves in these kinds of places. If it's windy and cloudy you'll have to blind cast. I seldom do well under these conditions.

Regardless of the starting water temperature, if the water warms three or four degrees during the day, you ought to find some feeding fish. If the wind isn't blowing you can frequently find the best tailing action of the year, and this is true in the entire Indian River Lagoon system- the Indian River Lagoon, the Mosquito Lagoon, and the Banana River Lagoon, especially in the no motor zone. In the NMZ you may well find giant reds and black drum tailing together in hip deep water (be still my heart!). Again, the circumstances are, late afternoon, calm conditions, bright sun all day.

Spring

Spring in the lagoon system doesn't last long. Warming water changes the behavior patterns of the fish, and frequently they become hard to find. Trout leave their shallow water locales, and sight fishing for them is over for the year. Black drum become occasional flats visitors instead of an expected target. Redfish schools tend to break up (although you can find schools of redfish any day of the year).

On the bright side, snook become more active. Crevalle start to show. The power stations south of Titusville open to fishing on April 1, and tarpon can frequently be found there along with hordes of ladyfish and sometimes jacks. Along the beach the manta rays are migrating, and with them are numbers of cobia. The monster jacks start showing up off the beaches, and there can be little doubt that the pogies, and the king mackerel, aren't far off.

Summer

Spring quickly gives way to summer. Afternoon thunderstorms start up, chasing anglers off the water. An early start is your best approach to fishing anywhere along the Space Coast at this time of year. Fishing at night can be a clever strategy.

There are two major weather features at this time of year. The first is the sea breeze, which can kick in at any time after about 9 am. What happens is that heating of the earth's surface by the sun warms the air above, which becomes less dense and begins to rise. Cooler air off the water moves in to replace the heated air. This cooler air is in turn heated and it rises.

All this rising air contains plenty of moisture. Cumulus clouds form as the rising air reaches the altitude where it hits its dew point. With sufficient lift and sufficient moisture, afternoon thunderstorms form. Sufficient lift and moisture are frequently achieved, since afternoon thunderstorms can be a daily occurrence all along the Space Coast during the summer months.

Tarpon, snook, and crevalle are all active at this time of year. Lagoon tarpon might range from babies of ten pounds to full figured specimens in triple digits weight-wise. Ocean tarpon are almost all big ones, averaging about 100 pounds. Snook can be found in the inlets and at the Port, along the beaches, and under shady residential docks in the lower half of the lagoon system. Crevalle might be anywhere, since they swim fast and cover lots of territory in their never ending search for bait. Look for showering mullet and multiple crashes and you have found yourself a school of hungry crevalle. Break out the surface plugs and have a blast!

Reds and trout are still available in the lagoons. Live pigfish become a prime bait for gator trout. Pigfish make good bait for almost any species in the lagoon, actually. Reds will tail at first light until the sea breeze kicks in, when they usually move off the flats into adjacent deeper water.

In the ocean, in addition to the tarpon, king mackerel make an excellent target for anglers. Big crevalle and sharks of many different species and all different sizes will crash the kingfish party, too. When fishing the Atlantic at this time of year you really need to be ready for anything in terms of fish size, as you will encounter fish of all sizes.

As summer winds down, the most major fishing event of the year starts- the annual run of finger mullet through the lagoons and along the beaches. The start of the mullet run signals yet another change of season.

Autumn

By the time of the Autumnal Equinox the mullet run is in full swing. The lagoons are full of mullet, and along the beaches the water is black with them. The weather is usually delightful, the water temperatures are in the comfort range of a wide variety of fish, and frequently the fishing is as good as it ever gets around here. It's my favorite time of year.

I detailed the beach mullet run in the previous chapter. In the lagoons, savvy anglers look for a school of nervous mullet and then follow them using either a pushpole of an electric motor. Gamefish of all kinds shadow these mullet schools, so working the bait schools frequently results in some excellent fishing.

It often pays to try to ambush gamefish by prowling at any of the funnel points in the lagoon system. For example, at every causeway the mullet have to swim out and around the fill upon which the road was built, passing through much deeper water than the shallow flats where they prefer to travel. Large fish wait to ambush them at these places. You should do the same. Points of land sticking out into the lagoon system act in the same manner, and are likewise excellent places to fish. Any canals extending from the shoreline out into the river offer larger fish an excellent ambush point. In other words, any structure that offers large fish an easy location to pick off a meal will likely be a good place to fish.

Frozen mullet make an excellent bait. If you have space in a freezer this is the best time to stock up, since by Thanksgiving most of the mullet are gone. They'll be scarce until it warms up again, sometime around Easter.

When the last of the mullet are gone, so too are the tarpon, most of the jacks, and most of the snook. Then the cycle repeats itself, somehow always repeating but never quite the same.

Photo 1- Ponce de Leon Inlet to Edgewater

Overview

According to my somewhat arbitrary designation, the Space Coast starts at Ponce de Leon Inlet (in Volusia County) and continues south to Sebastian Inlet (at the county line between Brevard and Indian River Counties) a distance of roughly 80 miles. The section of beach covered in this section (Photo 1, that is) runs from the jetty south to the entrance of Canaveral National Seashore. The beachfront property here is all developed. You can drive right onto the beach from a large number of access points off of SR A1A, fishing from the truck or launching small boats right into the surf.

On the inland side, the Intracoastal Waterway (ICW) forms the main channel through the backcountry, but numerous other creeks will be found. The tidal flow is quite significant here and heavily influences the fishing. It also influences the navigation once you leave the ICW. There are lots of islands, lots of oysters, and you can get into trouble fast. Always navigate with care.

The Jetties

Ponce Inlet connects the Indian River Lagoon system and Halifax River lagoon to the Atlantic. A jetty on the south side of the inlet forms the northern terminus of New Smyrna Beach. Another jetty on the north side of the inlet lies at the southern end of Daytona Beach.

Any time can provide good fishing on the jetties, but the best time to fish there is during the fall mullet run. This run typically begins toward the end of August and lasts into October. While the mullet are there the angler can catch a wide variety of gamefishes. Redfish, often big bulls over thirty pounds, follow the mullet, as do bluefish. The blues will sometimes be choppers, ten and twelve pounds. Tarpon and snook may be found there, as well as sharks of all sizes. Big doormat flounder and jack crevalle up to the thirty pound range also appear.

Local charter captain Kent Gibbens suggests using big tackle but traveling light if fishing on either jetty during the mullet run. Big tackle means a surfcasting rod of ten or twelve feet, with a spinning reel capable of handling 250 yards of seventeen pound test monofilament line. A ten foot shock leader of fifty to one hundred pound test (depending on the species desired or present) completes the outfit.

Kent also believes all tackle should be carried on one's person so at least one hand stays free for clambering on rocks which may be slick. A small backpack could carry all lures and rigs, although this might be hard to do if live mullet were the bait of choice. A burlap sack can be used to carry fish for the lucky angler who wants a fish dinner.

Kent suggests that jetty anglers wear old golf shoes with metal cleats, which supply superior traction on slick rocks. They help prevent falls and could save a big fish or your life. Falling into the water during a strong outgoing tide could be very hazardous, especially if you're stunned after bouncing off a few boulders.

During the mullet run live mullet make a superior bait, and can be captured with a castnet right from the beach. They can be livelined on a single hook, or weighted down with a sliding egg sinker rig, depending on where the fish are feeding.

Large poppers cast into the surf will also work well. Large here means three, four, or five ounces. If the big blues or sharks are around, use a foot of wire leader to prevent cutoffs.

Once the mullet run is over the fishing is not. Redfish prowl the jetties all year, although not in the sizes or concentrations they attain during the run. Like reds everywhere, they take a variety of baits and lures. Finger mullet, crabs, and shrimp are all effective naturals, usually fished near or right on the bottom.

Sheepshead will always be found at the jetties. The largest fish come in during the winter. Shrimp work well, although fiddler crabs are probably the best bait. Successful sheepshead fishermen need nothing more elaborate than a cane pole for tackle. With a sinker and a baited hook, the bait is worked close to the rocks. Regardless of the tackle used, keep the bait probing in the holes close to the rocks.

Another fish found in the area during the colder months and into the spring is the Spanish mackerel. The Spanish advertise their presence by chasing glass minnows or other small forage up to the surface. Terns and other birds join the fracas, tipping off the anglers that the mackerel are in. Using small jigs or spoons with a 30 pound fluorocarbon leader can quickly lead to a limit catch. Expect some cutoffs.

Small blues averaging a pound or three hang around the jetties most of the winter as well. I've seen them so thick that catching two at a time on a single Mirr-O-Lure was the rule rather than the exception. Catching them under these circumstances is anything but challenging.

For those looking for a challenge, divers claim snook stack up under the north jetty all year. They are seldom caught by anglers. Obviously if the fish are living there they must be eating, so why are they such an uncommon catch? The secret of taking Ponce snook consistently is waiting to be discovered by the angler who innovates and perseveres.

Flounder come in whenever bait is plentiful, usually beginning sometime in July and staying through the end of the mullet run. Pompano are another prized summer catch. Whiting are in the surf around the jetties all year. Black drum ranging in size from puppies to enormous are taken from the jetties, particularly during the winter. They prefer clams or crabs, but fellows tossing shrimp take their share.

Regardless of what rig you may use, bring lots of extras. The bottom is full of rocky snags that eat rigs like crazy. If you're not prepared to re-rig, you will not be fishing very long.

Along the Beach

Sometime after the middle of August, and extending into October during a good year, the annual run of mullet heading south along the coast passes the entire Space Coast. One man who has taken advantage of the run for year after year is Kent Gibbens, a lifelong resident of the Daytona Beach area. Kent shared his insights into the spectacular fishing available then.

For the beach-bound angler who wants truly big fish, this time of the year should not be missed. Big bluefish, jumbo reds, whopper jack crevalle, sharks, tarpon, an occasional snook,

Ponce de Leon Inlet

Ponce de Leon Cut

New Smyrna Beach

ICW

Smyrna Creek

SR 44

Public Boat Ramp

South Causeway

Calalisa Creek

and once in a great while even a kingfish will be caught from the beach.

Kent prefers artificials for this fishing, claiming that dealing with bait is too time-consuming. Carrying those mullet also cuts down on an angler's mobility. Kent likes poppers, three, four, even five ounce models. Obviously, a big bait like this necessitates a big surf stick, whether spinning or conventional. It must work- Kent still holds the 12 pound line class world record for spotted seatrout with a 14 pound fish he caught on a big Atom Popper back in 1972.

The general idea is to find a pod of bait, especially nervous bait, and keep flinging the popper in and around the pod. The bait is nervous for a reason, and the popper should find the cause before too long.

Kent says the absolute best fishing of the year is also the toughest- a northeast wind at night during the mullet run, usually around the end of September or the beginning of October. He mourns the passing of night beach driving, saying that not being able to drive keeps fishermen off of the beach during the best possible fishing times.

For those anglers for whom flinging heavy poppers on big tackle gets to be too much like work, live baiting with mullet will certainly account for fish. Titusville angler Terry Friedrichs told me he saw a 120 pound tarpon taken from the beach last summer during the mullet run on a live mullet. Frozen mullet are more convenient and sometimes just as effective.

When the mullet aren't running plenty of other fishing is available from the beach. Whiting are almost always there. A light spinning rod with a couple of one-eighth to one quarter ounce bucktail jigs tied in tandem and tipped with a piece of shrimp can be deadly.

Pompano are another prized beach fish, although they are not nearly as reliable as the whiting. Pompano seem to travel in order to stay in areas where their favorite food, the mole crab or sand flea, is abundant. Fish for them like you would for whiting, or use a long surf stick with light line so you can cast out beyond the first bar.

Speaking of sand fleas, when they are available they make an excellent and easily caught bait for most beach fish. You can just dig a few holes at the water line and see if you find any, or buy (or make) a sand flea scooper, a kind of small wire basket on a handle. Sand fleas can be simply pierced with a bait hook, or used to tip a bucktail jig.

Black drum and sometimes redfish also range the beach. Redfish feed pretty opportunistically, but black drum greatly prefer crustaceans (shrimp or crabs) or clams.

Bluefish are found along the beach all winter. Cut mullet, whether fresh or frozen, works as well as anything else you could use.

One fact that Volusia County's tourist development board doesn't advertise is that Volusia beaches have one of the country's largest number of human-shark interactions every year. Fortunately most bites require nothing more than a few stitches. But sharks of all sizes constantly patrol this stretch of beach. Any kind of fish can be used for shark bait, but mullet, pogies, and ladyfish all work particularly well.

Crevalle, tarpon, and flounder can also be caught from the beach, and boaters can get off the beach a ways into more tarpon and kingfish as well.

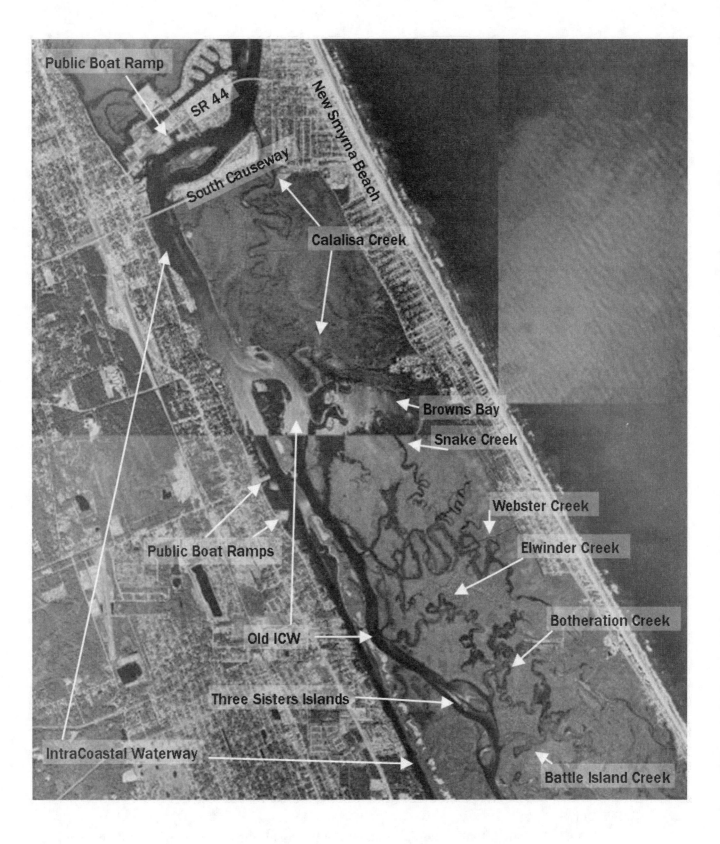

Public Boat Ramp

SR 44

South Causeway

New Smyrna Beach

Calalisa Creek

Browns Bay

Snake Creek

Webster Creek

Elwinder Creek

Public Boat Ramps

Botheration Creek

Old ICW

Three Sisters Islands

IntraCoastal Waterway

Battle Island Creek

Before arbitrarily picking a fishing spot on the beach, look for a few moments at the way the waves are breaking from as high a vantage point as you can find. You want to find the holes and run-outs on the nearshore bar that will concentrate fish.

If you intend to fish along this stretch of beach keep in mind that it can be heavily used by bathers and surfers, especially on summer weekends. Try to get your fishing in early or late in the day so you can avoid all the traffic.

In The Lagoon System
Access
East Side- there are no boat ramps on the east side in this stretch. Canoeists or kayakers can launch at Calalisa Park, by the SR 44 bridge over Calalisa Creek.
West Side- There is a good public ramp off of SR 44 in New Smyrna Beach. There is a good public ramp across from City Hall, on Park Avenue off of US 1 in Edgewater. There is a private ramp at Cameron's Marina, on the south side of Edgewater, on Boston Road off of US 1.

Fishing Here- West Side
Between the SR 40 bridge in the city of Ormond Beach and the town Oak Hill the Intra-coastal Waterway (ICW) wends its way for almost thirty miles. In that distance it passes by one inlet, under seven bridges, by ten or so communities, dozens of creeks, hundreds of docks, and thousands of islands and oyster shoals. The ICW itself provides habitat for many popular sport fish- redfish, snook, seatrout, flounder, tarpon, jack crevalle, bluefish, sheepshead, whiting, black drum, and others.

In spite of the largely urban character of this area, you can go off the ICW only a short distance and feel as though you're in a remote area. Even along the ICW itself, the bridges, oysters, and seawalls provide plenty of habitat for "urban" fish. Ponce Inlet provides a conduit for ocean-going fish seeking to feed on the area's plentiful shrimp and baitfish. We will look at the many opportunities anglers have for fishing this area, including piers and bridges, wading, and from a boat.

Like the rest of the fisheries down the Space Coast, this one changes seasonally. The snook and tarpon of summer give way to bluefish as the days grow short and the water cools off. Reds and trout remain all year however, and many anglers favor the colder months for these two species.

Snook and tarpon are the glamour species of the area. The snook and tarpon can be really hard to catch. The anglers I spoke to (Captain Ron Rebeck of Debary, Captain Kent Gibbens of Ormond Beach, and Captain Fred Hill of Edgewater) who claim to have good success with these species all use the same technique. They fish around structure from a boat, usually after sunset.

Excellent night fishing opportunities exist by the bridges and under lighted docks all the way from J.B.'s Fish Camp in New Smyrna to Tomoka State Park in Ormond Beach. Moonfish (near the inlet), snook, seatrout, jack crevalle, and ladyfish are all likely catches. Tarpon are never really likely, but remain a constant possibility.

The docks along the Intracoastal from Edgewater north to Ormond Beach will hold such fish as snook, seatrout, tarpon, and redfish. The best docks are old and beat up, with a lot of barnacles, oysters, and other such growth on them. Look for a good current flow under a dock that can't support the weight of a human any more and there's a strong possibility it will hold fish. The least productive docks are new, or have bait buckets hanging off of them.

Fred Hill says, "Most of the time the bigger snook will be right under the dock, as you might expect. But big gator trout will often lie out away from the dock, sometimes as far away as 10 feet." Although the snook action slows during the colder months, these big trout remain and feed all winter long. Regardless of the species or season, Hill prefers jigs for this type of fishing, with the deep running DOA Bait Buster (he calls it the "rubber mullet") being a favorite. He says you need to fish these lures slowly, right on the bottom.

Kent Gibbens adds that in order to fish the docks or the bridges with any degree of consistent success a quiet approach is essential. He says a powerful trolling motor or an efficient anchoring system is necessary to stay in the strike zone. Drifting works poorly or not at all.

During the summer both tarpon and snook can be taken between the two bridges in New Smyrna on a rising tide, after the clean seawater comes in. Successful anglers use swimming plugs like the Bomber Long A, or live finger mullet. Fly fishers can try using standard tarpon streamers. All of the bridges in this area can produce both snook and tarpon during the summer months. Most successful anglers fish from boats. It's not that the folks on the bridges don't hook up, but they have a hard time controlling an 80 pound tarpon from the bridge!

You can certainly catch fish here during the daylight hours, too. The same docks that produce fish at night will also yield catches during the day. Channels funneling between islands or oyster bars, creek mouths, seawalls, pilings, and other structure usually attract and hold fish.

There is an unmarked channel that more or less parallels the ICW from roughly marker 47 in Edgewater south all the way to Packwood Place, by marker 67. This channel provides some excellent fishing opportunities and allows for fairly safe navigation. When water drains from Big and Little Snapper cuts, the funnel effect will of course attract fish, and this is true of every creek mouth in this stretch. Any shorelines with adjacent deep water can and will hold fish, particularly during cold weather.

Fishing Here- East Side

If you fish from a powerboat a visit here is not for the faint of heart. Oysters are ubiquitous, and will chew up your gel coat and lower unit in a nanosecond. This is a great area to use a hand powered craft such as a canoe or kayak, although wading spots are rare.

Calalisa Creek runs from just north of the South Bridge in New Smyrna Beach south all the way to Browns Bay, east of the public boat ramp in Edgewater. Water depth in the creek ranges from none to over five feet, depending on where you are and the tide. Redfish, seatrout, snapper, sheepshead, and some black drum are permanent residents, and the usual summer fish can be found in season. The creek's character is formed by oyster bars and mangroves with deeper holes, and most of the creek can and will hold fish. This is a great place for a hand powered boat, as it's lightly traveled by motor vessels.

Browns Bay lies almost due east of the public ramp in Edgewater. It's a beautiful piece of water, frequently has someone fishing it, and frequently holds both trout and redfish.

Snake Creek runs south from Browns Bay almost all the way to JB's Fish Camp. You'll have to be lucky and have high water to navigate this creek. Although I'm sure there must be someone out there who's done this, I haven't met anyone who has. It's a personal goal of mine.

There is a lot of water that holds a lot of fish in this area. Explore it and have some fun.

Photo 2- Mosquito Lagoon, Edgewater to Oak Hill

Overview

This section of the Mosquito Lagoon is much like the previous one. Lots of islands, creeks, and channels create a watery maze that is chock full of fish habitat. According to Capt. Mike Hakala, north of a line running roughly from the Eldora House on the eastern side to the River Breeze Park on the west, the water tends to be turbid. You'll find considerable tidal flow, lots of oysters, and relatively little seagrass. South of this line the current, while still present, starts to peter out. The oysters become much less abundant, and the water tends to be clearer. Clear water allows seagrasses to grow.

Remember that during the winter months cold fronts knock down a lot of the phytoplankton that grows in the water during the summer months. The water is much cleaner then.

Remember also that the redfish tend to school up during the winter, and the trout will often get into very shallow water to sun themselves.

Because of all the oysters in this area jonboats and other flat bottomed skiffs are quite popular here. Hand powered vessels such as canoes and kayaks also make a lot of sense. Few of the backcountry passages are marked, and because of all the oysters and expanses of very shallow water, motor vessel navigation anywhere off of the ICW can be treacherous.

The Intracoastal Waterway runs along the western shoreline the entire length of this section. The Old Channel, described earlier, runs roughly in a northwest-southeast line, cutting diagonally across this region to reach the eastern shoreline just north of Turtle Mound.

This north part of this section of the Mosquito Lagoon lies outside the boundaries of the Canaveral National Seashore. Everything west of the ICW and south of a line running roughly northeast from Turtle Mound on the eastern shoreline, following the Shipyard Canal and the Old Channel to a line that runs due east of a point between ICW markers 62 and 63, lies within the boundaries of Canaveral National Seashore. The National Seashore is administered by the National Park Service, and there are NPS backcountry campsites on many of the islands back here. You must have a backcountry permit to camp at any of these sites. These permits are available at the Turtle Mound Ranger Station (386.428.3384x10).

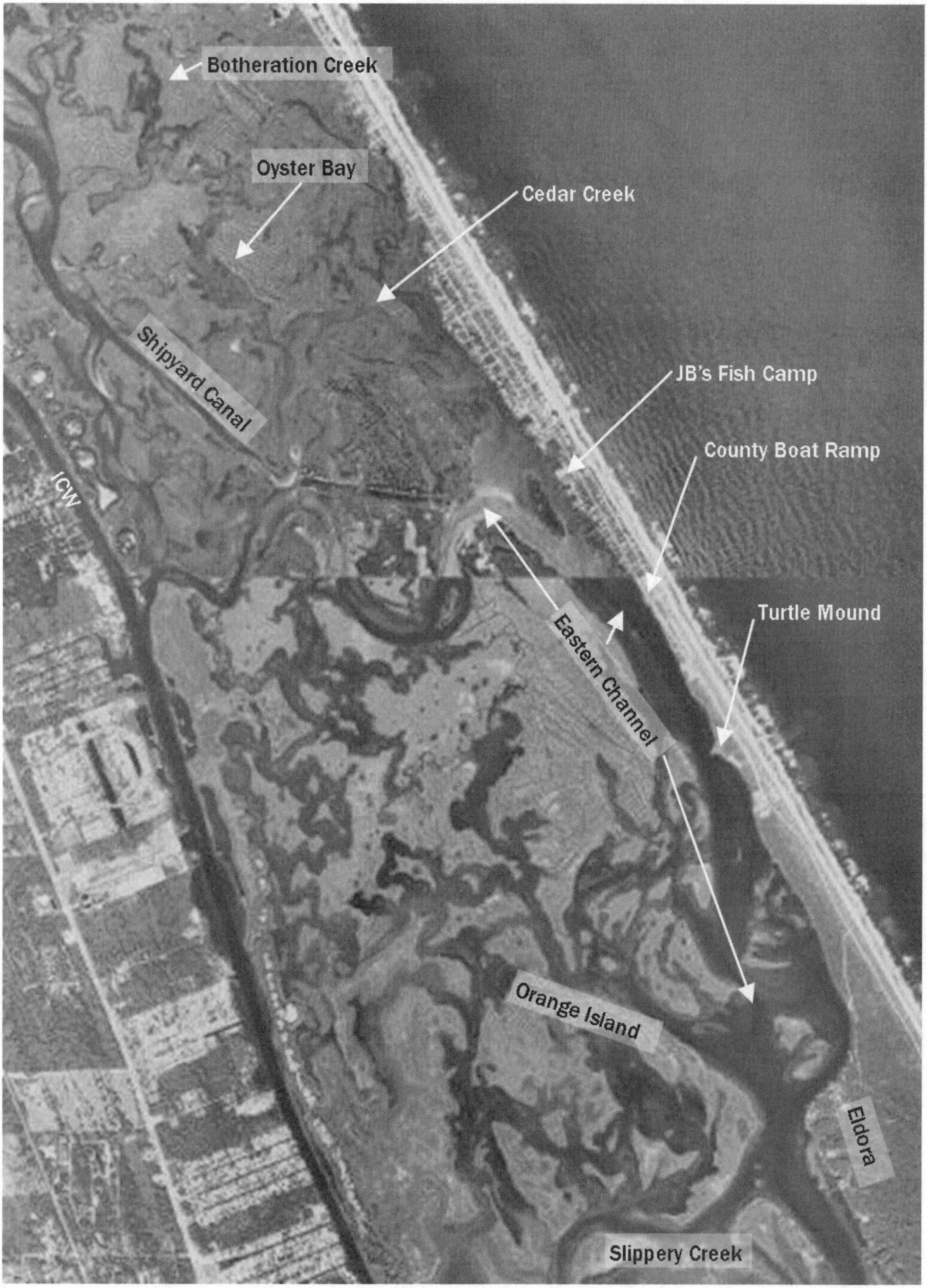

Botheration Creek

Oyster Bay

Cedar Creek

Shipyard Canal

ICW

JB's Fish Camp

County Boat Ramp

Turtle Mound

Eastern Channel

Orange Island

Eldora

Slippery Creek

A word about JB's Fish Camp- JB's is a fixture in the social scene in this area. They serve excellent food, ice cold beverages, and usually have a band and a big party going on every weekend. If you're fishing anywhere in this area it's worth stopping by for a visit and a snack.

Access

On the east side along SR A1A you will find JB's Fish Camp, a private facility that charges a fee; and the Volusia County Public Ramp, between JB's and Turtle Mound.

On the west side there are a series of fish camps from Edgewater south, accessed from US 1: Cameron's Marina; Bissitte Bay Fish Camp; Indian Mound Fish Camp; Lopez Fish Camp; and LeFil's Fish Camp. All of these ramps are private and charge a launch fee. Some sell bait and tackle items as well. River Breeze Park, off of US 1 just north of the town of Oak Hill, is a Volusia County public ramp and is an excellent facility.

Fishing Here- West Side

As already mentioned, the ICW runs the length of this section along the developed western shoreline. Waterfront development means docks, and docks usually mean fish. These docks are especially productive after dark. The ones with lights are the ones to fish, and the better ones will have fish visibly feeding around them. See the last section for tactics.

The ICW itself will have fish in and along it. There's a lot of boat traffic, but this entire stretch of the ICW between Cameron's Marina (marker 56) and LeFil's Fish Camp (marker 9A) is a slow speed zone. This makes fishing this stretch somewhat more tolerable.

Kent Gibbens says that along the west shoreline there's quite a bit of Spartina grass which holds a lot of trout and redfish. Kent likes to fish the edges of this grass with jigs tipped with shrimp and says he does quite well.

Mentioned in the last section was the old ICW channel, which roughly parallels the current channel from marker 47 in Edgewater south to the Shipyard Canal. At that point the canal runs off to the southeast and a natural channel runs off to the southwest, where it rejoins the ICW near marker 67. The area of this channel around the Three Sisters Islands produces a lot of big summer tarpon for the patient and early rising angler. Deep water shorelines on the east side of this channel south of Three Sisters produce trout and reds, and sometimes snook. And of course any cut where water flows out forms a funnel that will attract and hold all kinds of fish.

Bissitte Bay, just to the east of ICW marker 75, can be very productive for both redfish and seatrout. Slippery Creek runs out of the southeast corner of Bissitte Bay and winds its way over to the east side of the lagoon coming out by Pumpkin Point and the Eldora House. This entire creek can hold fish, as can all the adjoining creeks and bays.

The bay east of the spoil islands between ICW markers 8 and 9A is another good area for both seatrout and redfish. The waters around an island known as Hong Kong Island are frequently worth taking a few minutes to explore. Sometimes hundreds of redfish school up here.

Fishing Here- East Side

The east side for our purposes is pretty much everything east of the immediate vicinity of the ICW. And if you spend much time in here poking around there are a whole lot of places you may turn up a fish or two.

Running north and south from JB's Fish Camp is a channel. Just west of this channel, across from JB's, is a good sized flat which can offer good redfish action.

Cedar Creek, north of JB's, can produce a variety of fish including trout, reds, drum, snapper, sheepshead, and more. Drift the creek with live shrimp, or blind-cast with any good lure that will cover a lot of water. Jigs tipped with shrimp can be particularly effective.

The creeks and bays to the north of Cedar Creek and east of the Shipyard Canal also offer a lot of productive water. Deeper holes offer fish a thermal refuge during cold weather and frequently stack up with trout. As has been stated previously, it's easy to get in trouble here in a fast moving powerboat because of the oysters. Use caution while navigating. There are a lot of nooks and crannies that beg for exploration from hand powered boats.

At Turtle Mound is a deep hole that will hold fish, especially trout, in cold weather. Unfortunately the productivity of this hole has declined considerably in recent years.

A short distance to the southwest of Turtle Mound, between Shipyard Island and Orange Island, is a shallow area full of oyster bars which often produces redfish and seatrout. Again, this is a poling area unless you want to power into oysters. All the islands and creeks to the west of here offer lots of opportunities for exploration from a shallow draft boat. I love to kayak and wade this entire area, and frequently do quite well here.

The shoreline and docks to the northeast of the Eldora House is a well-known winter seatrout spot. Again, and sadly, the productivity of this area has declined in recent years. The islands north of this shore line, known as Raggedy Gap, can produce reds and sometimes trout.

The fact is, all the creeks and islands in this area can hold fish. If you study the aerial photos carefully you will find some deeper areas (Gaines Slough, for example) that offer refuge to the fish when they move off the flats. My best advice is to explore and learn the area a little bit at a time, and it will provide a lifetime of quality angling for you.

The Beach- Canaveral National Seashore

Canaveral National Seashore contains about 23 miles of fabulously undeveloped beach, the last such stretch on the east coast of Florida. On the west side of this narrow spit of land lies the Mosquito Lagoon. With such a wealth of fertile waters surrounding them, it is no wonder that the area's natives easily survived on fish and shellfish to the extent that they were able to build shell mounds on the order of Turtle Mound. Due to its large size it was used as a navigational aid by Spanish and English ships servicing settlers in the New World.

Today, anglers find a wide variety of choices facing them when they visit this area. On the ocean side, pompano, whiting, black drum, Spanish mackerel, redfish, flounder, bluefish, sharks, crevalle, even tarpon, can all be caught from the beach during the right season.

At the north end of the National Seashore, the ocean side is known as Apollo Beach. Access is from S.R. A1A south out of New Smyrna. Five parking areas fill up quickly on summer weekends, but are generally ample during the rest of the year, especially for early risers. The National Park Service allows overnight camping south of Parking Lot 5 for those willing to carry in everything they'll need; however access is limited to between November and May. Nesting sea turtles during the summer and fall months need protection from human interference, so night access is prohibited during that time.

The beach fishery changes along with the seasons, but regardless of the time of year greater success goes to those with a strategy. Beach fishing regular Jim Manley gave me several tips for placing baits in the high percentage zone.

Manley prefers fishing by parking lot 4, feeling that there's less traffic from bathers and surfers there. Before he ever rigs a line, he walks to the top of the boardwalk over the dunes and surveys the waters below for holes, sloughs, and run-outs along the beach. Since he often fishes in the morning, the low angle of the sun prevents him from seeing the bottom directly. The breaking of the waves give him the information he needs.

Jim says that these beach features hold fish because bait concentrates there. Once he knows where to cast, he rigs his tackle up at his car before walking down onto the beach. This idea is a good one, as it helps keep sand out of the reels and rod ferrules.

Jim also says that less stuff on your line is better. Regardless of what the target species, use the thinnest line, the smallest hooks, the lightest sinkers, and the thinnest leaders you can. Avoid the use of swivels whenever possible. Use only the bare necessities and you will get more hookups. More hookups usually means more fish caught.

Manley usually carries two rods, a 12 footer for power casts out past the offshore bar, and a 10 foot finesse rod for the nearshore sloughs. He prefers to use live or fresh dead shrimp for bait. Fish eat them, they're usually available, and he thinks it's less trouble than digging sand fleas. Manley makes his own two hook pompano rigs, claiming self made are superior to what's available commercially. When he puts the shrimp on the hook, he adds a little twist that I had never seen before.

Like lots of other fishermen, Manley breaks off the tail flipper and inserts the hook point through the hole made there. But then he squeezes the head of the shrimp, forcing all of the juices from the head back into the body. He then pulls the head off. Jim claims that the shrimp release more scent into the water this way, which results in more strikes.

For the fisherman who wants drum, clams or cut crabs are always good bait, perhaps even better than shrimp.

Sinker size depends on the size of the surf, and ranges on these big surf sticks between three and five ounces. Jim prefers four ounce sinkers, and says if you need to go to a six ounce weight fishing will probably be pretty bad.

Ace Hardaway fishes for pompano. He's so good at it, he makes his living hook-and-lining pompano commercially. He does things a little differently than does Jim Manley. During the winter months he uses a 15 foot rod. He spools up with twelve pound line but uses a 20 foot shock leader of 25-30 pound fluorocarbon. Casting it a mile is important in the winter, according to Ace, since the fish will often hold well off of the beach. Also, the length of the rod helps to keep the line up above the breakers, so less weight is needed to hold the bottom.

Like Manley, Ace like to fish the holes, run-outs, and sloughs along the beach. He scouts the beach at dead low tide, then comes back to fish during the higher water stages.

All year long Hardaway prefers sand fleas for bait, so much so that he will drive over 100 miles one way to dig up a fresh supply for a day's fishing. He feels shrimp or frozen fleas are a distant second to live fleas for pompano.

During the warmer months he puts away the 15 foot surf stick and takes out an ultralight spinning rod. The fish hold right in among the breakers looking for fleas, and that's where he catches them, oftentimes by sight fishing if water clarity and the sun's angle permit it.

Hardaway often fishes at Playalinda Beach, and prefers the higher number parking lots since there's less traffic there. During summer he likes to fish from first light to about 8:00 AM, and will often catch whiting and sometimes big redfish while casting for pompano.

Photo 3- Mosquito Lagoon, Oak Hill to County Line

Overview
This section of the Mosquito Lagoon features mostly open water, with grass flats rimming the edges. To the west of the ICW are a string of spoil islands, often referred to as clinkers (all waters west of the ICW are within a slow speed manatee zone). Inside the clinkers is a long, relatively narrow strip of grass flats.

South and east of Oak Hill a sand bar known as Georges Bank runs most of the way across the lagoon towards parking lot 5 at Canaveral National Seashore. This bar has no markers on it except for a single PVC pipe at the west end. North of Georges Bank lie more grass flats. On the south side of the bar the water is fairly deep (by lagoon standards).

On the east side of the lagoon, a sand bar that marks the western edge of the grass flats runs mostly unbroken roughly north and south from just south of the boat ramp at the National Seashore parking lot 5 all the way down south of Preachers Island. Where it comes closest to the ICW (at marker 25) it is known as Tiger Shoals. A metal pipe marks a break in this bar at the south end of Tiger Shoals, due east of ICW marker 27. Other than this, such breaks as there are in this bar are for the most part unmarked, making navigation over the bar treacherous, especially when the light is bad.

The Volusia/Brevard county line runs east and west across the lagoon from just north of ICW channel marker 29 to a point due east, just north of Three Cabbage Island.

Access
On the west side of the lagoon you'll find a boat ramp at LeFils Fish Camp in Oak Hill (fee required). They have restrooms, sell bait, and your vehicle will be safe here.

Farther south by marker 29 is a National Wildlife Refuge ramp. It's a small dirt ramp suitable only for car top boats, jonboats, etc., and also provides some wading access. Break-ins to vehicles parked here has been an ongoing problem.

On the east side of the lagoon there is a dirt ramp suitable only for small boats at parking lot 5 at Canaveral National Seashore. There is a fee required for entrance to the Seashore, and the rangers enforce the speed laws rigorously.

Fishing Here- North Side

Georges Bank is a very fishy looking piece of water, but sometimes it is completely barren. On the other hand it can be every bit as good as it looks. It's a great place to wade, with a very hard bottom.

Reds and trout both use the bar. By poling along you can sightfish both species up along the edge or even on top of the bar. Blind casting from the bar will also produce trout. Trout fishermen like to fish this area with live pigfish during the summer months.

Jacks and bluefish will also use the bar, pinning schools of mullet against it. This happens infrequently, but it is awesome when it happens.

There is a large school (+/- 200 fish) of large redfish that periodically show up along this bar. While sometimes their appearance is fleeting, other times they stay there for weeks. The word quickly gets out and the fish are mercilessly hounded. You almost feel sorry for them. Look for the fleet of boats and the fish will be in the middle of it.

Fishing Here- West Side

The grass flats behind the clinkers from LeFils Fish Camp all the way to the Haulover Canal will hold both trout and redfish. You need to look for areas with deep water access between the islands. You will seldom find fish behind islands that are joined together by bars. Wading here is tough. The flats are just hard enough to wade, but plenty soft enough that you will get stuck, fall down, and otherwise give your legs a great workout.

Trout and reds also work along the outside edge of these flats and all along the spoil islands. Due to boat traffic in the ICW I don't enjoy casting jigs for trout on the channel side of the islands, but I see plenty of people who do. They catch a lot of fish. Wading along the clinkers is enjoyable, too, as the bottom here is quite firm.

During the winter months grouper fishermen troll large swimming plugs in the channel, another form of fishing which I do not enjoy. Again, they are sometimes quite successful. If you want to do this, concentrate your efforts in front of those spoil islands with rocky shorelines.

Fishing Here- East Side

Some of Mosquito Lagoon's best areas are located here. Having said that, many of the grass flats inside the bar are extremely shallow. I see many folks back there in boats that have no business being there. These people are usually stuck, throwing up mud and tearing up the grass in their attempts to get out. Use extreme caution when navigating around here.

If you do not have a shallow running boat equipped with power trim and tilt you have no business running behind Tiger Shoals or into any other of the lagoon's shallow areas!

In many places it's also too shallow for electric motor use. Up on these flats the

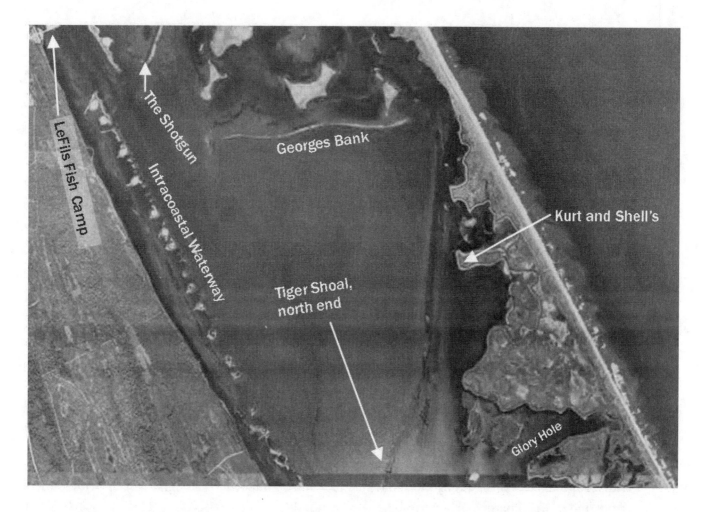

LeFils Fish Camp

The Shotgun

Intracoastal Waterway

Georges Bank

Kurt and Shell's

Tiger Shoal,
north end

Glory Hole

A view of the north end of the Mosquito Lagoon basin. LeFils Fish Camp is in the extreme upper left corner. The bar that snakes east to west near the top of the photo is Georges Bank. An excellent place to wade, this bar often holds fish. A school of big redfish sometimes remains here for weeks.

Running along the west side of the lagoon are spoil islands, formed from material dredged from the ICW. These islands, and the flats behind them, often hold both trout and redfish.

A clearly visible bar runs roughly north and south along the eastern side of the lagoon. Again, the edges of this bar and all the flats inside of it can be excellent producers of both trout and redfish.

pushpole is by far the best way, and many times the only way, to go.

All along this bar seatrout lurk. Deeper draft boats can fish these areas quite successfully. Redfish of all sizes also cruise along this bar, sometimes in singles, sometimes in big schools containing hundreds of individuals. Tiger Shoals, like Georges Bank, has a large school of big reds that shows up periodically, and like at Georges Bank they sometimes stay for weeks. Also like Georges Bank the word quickly circulates that they are there, and they get worked over very hard.

Behind the bar some areas to check include the shallow slough just south of the parking lot 5 boat ramp. This slough often holds trout, especially during the winter months. Look for them on white patches. Reds (legal sized ones) also get in here.

The point known as Shell and Kurt's also holds fish sometimes, as does the shallow bay to the south. This bay is so shallow that when the water is low you simply cannot get back there in any kind of boat.

The area around Bird Island and back up into the Glory Hole holds fish as consistently as anywhere in the lagoon. Thick grass means redfish tail there well sometimes, especially late in the day on warm, sunny winter afternoons.

The plane wrecks flat inside of Tiger Shoals is another area that sometimes holds hundreds of redfish and some very large trout. During the winter a large school of black drum sometimes gets up in there, too. This flat likewise is very shallow, especially at its north side. Expect to pole quite a ways when it's time to leave.

As mentioned earlier, there is a pipe marking the south end of Tiger Shoal. A slough runs from this pipe back along the south side of Vann's Island. This slough loads up with both trout and redfish, particularly during the winter months.

West of Preachers Island there is a bar running east and west, called appropriately enough East and West. Not very consistently this bar will hold fish. Trout and reds will use the white holes on the north side of it to sun themselves during the winter months.

The area around Preachers Island and east all the way into the back is very shallow, but holds fish sometimes. If you go back here expect to pole a long way back out again. There are no "escape holes" where you can get your boat up on plane anywhere.

Photo 4- Mosquito Lagoon, County Line to Cucumber Island

Overview

The character of the lagoon here is similar to what was described in the last section. Spoil islands with flats behind them run along the ICW channel from the county line south to the Haulover Canal. The flats continue south all the way the end of the lagoon but there are no more islands along the west side. There are, however, old residential canals that run across this flat back into the shoreline.

On the east side it's also much like what was described in the previous section. A bar runs roughly north and south along the edge of the grass flat, which extends east to the sand dunes of Canaveral National Seashore. This bar is mostly unmarked, zigzags quite a bit, and has only a few breaks. Navigate with caution.

Access

On the west side there is a National Wildlife Refuge concrete boat ramp at the site of the old Beacon 42 Fish Camp. They've obviously changed the markers, since the ramp is now by marker 39. Vehicle break-ins have been somewhat of a problem here.

On the Haulover Canal there is a National Wildlife Refuge concrete boat ramp. It handles only one boat at a time and gets very crowded on weekends. Vehicle break-ins have been somewhat of a problem here, too.

Roughly three miles south of the Haulover Canal on the west side there is a National Wildlife Refuge dirt boat ramp at the site of the old Atmospheric Research Station on Bio Lab Road. This ramp will handle small boats only. Vehicle break-ins have been somewhat of a problem here.

As of this writing, none of the National Wildlife Refuge ramps have any facilities whatsoever, not even trash cans.

There is no access on the east side of the lagoon in this section.

Fishing Here- West Side

The grass flats behind the clinkers from the county line all the way to the Haulover Canal will hold both trout and redfish. You need to look for areas with deep water access between the islands. You will seldom find fish behind islands that are joined together by bars.

Wading here is hard work. The flats are just firm enough to wade, but plenty soft enough that you will sometimes get stuck and fall down. If you wade here your legs, and heart, will get a great workout.

Trout and reds also work along the outside edge of these flats and all along the spoil islands. Due to boat traffic in the ICW I don't enjoy casting jigs for trout on the channel side of the islands, but I see plenty of people who do. They catch a lot of fish. Wading around these islands is enjoyable, too, as the bottom on the ICW side is quite firm.

At the end of the channel leading to Beacon 42 Fish Camp there's a bar and flat on the east side of the ICW. Reds and trout both use this flat, and sometimes big reds can be found on the deep water edge on the east side of this flat.

At the entrance to the Haulover Canal is a 20 foot plus hole where a lot of people bottom fish. Grouper are sometimes caught here during the winter, and a school of bull reds can come through at any time. Black drum and other species are taken here sometimes, too. In the canal itself the other popular spot for bottom fishers is at the fenders of the SR 3 bridge. Black drum and redfish are the primary species, but sheepshead are also caught. You never know what you might catch in the canal. I caught a Spanish mackerel in there one time.

South of the canal flats continue all the way to the south end of the lagoon. Wading access between the canal and the Research Station ramp is by boat only, and since the bottom is fairly soft it's tough going anyway. Both trout and reds will lie in the cuts of the old residential canals that were dug in this stretch, and can be found all along the flats here. Having said that (and even though I'm sure they must get in here sometimes), I have never seen a large school of reds in this area.

Less than a mile north of the Research Station ramp is a bar that runs north and south along the eastern edge of the flat, marked by two wooden two by fours (the "Goal Posts") that are right next to each other. Reds will sometimes congregate around this bar.

Fishing Here- East Side

Running south of Preachers Island the next point that you encounter is Three Cabbage Island. Redfish can sometimes be found on the flat between Preachers Island and Three Cabbage Island, but stopping here is a commitment. There's no easy way out except by pushpole.

Redfish can sometimes be found on any side of Three Cabbage Island. On the northeast side of Three Cabbage is a shallow cut. Don't try to run or even pole through here unless the water is way up, unless you like getting out of your boat and pushing it through deep mud.

South of Three Cabbage Island is a wide, shallow flat. If the water is up high enough to run east across here you will come into a slough that runs north and south along the shoreline. The entire slough is perhaps a mile long and has a white sand bottom. Fishing for trout and reds anywhere along here can sometimes be excellent, especially during the winter.

Out at the edge of the flat our friendly bar runs generally north and south, with many twists and turns. Fish can be anywhere on either side of the bar, and especially during the summer it's not uncommon to find big schools of fish out here. Big redfish can sometimes be found on the deep side of this bar.

This bar has a break in it to the northeast of the Haulover Canal, about due west of Pardon Island. If you run ENE from this break, just to the north of Pardon Island (sometimes called Twin Palms), you find yourself in another broad, sandy slough. Fish can be found on the flats all around the margin of this slough, all the way back towards the sand dunes.

Running still farther south from Pardon Island you'll see a single small island, and then two islands that are quite close together. All of these islands can have fish around them. To the south and west of the pair of islands is a complex permutation in our bar, which forms a distinct

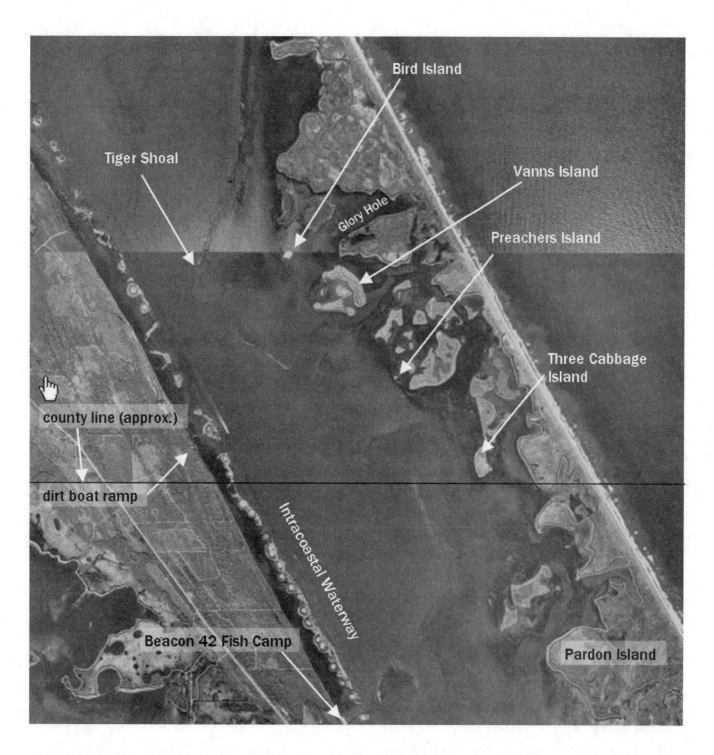

Tiger Shoal, an extension of the north-south bar shown in the previous photo, is one of the best known landmarks in the Mosquito Lagoon. Although any place in the lagoon can be barren of fish periodically, Tiger Shoal is as consistent a producer of fish as can be found here. Boats not equipped with power trim and tilt, or boats not designed to float in inches of water, have no business getting on this flat, though. At normal water levels most of it is about a foot deep.

Shallow draft boaters will have fun exploring all the nooks and crannies around all the islands on the eastern shoreline. Miles of shallow grassflats await those who enjoy using a pushpole.

elbow here, bending off to the east. Deep water lies on the south side of the bar, and fish of all sizes can frequently be found here.

Still further to the west of the elbow bar and its surrounding deeper water is yet another flat and bar, almost in the middle of the lagoon and southeast of the Haulover Canal. The bar runs for nearly a mile in a NW/SE orientation. The flat behind this bar sometimes holds both reds and trout.

OK, back to those two small islands. If you're near these two islands the water is fairly shallow, with thick manatee grass and some sizeable white holes on the bottom. You can pole due east to a point right along the sand dunes (you can clearly hear the surf on the beach here) and then follow the flat south all the way to Cucumber Island. Both reds and trout use the shoreline and nearby white spots. There is one small point along this piece of shoreline, with water deep enough at the tip to put a flats boat up on plane.

Sizeable schools of reds frequently utilize the flats south of here all the way to Cucumber Island. This flat is large, though, and there is no other place to plane up anywhere on it except for the edge or in the just mentioned hole. Stopping here represents a commitment unless the water is high.

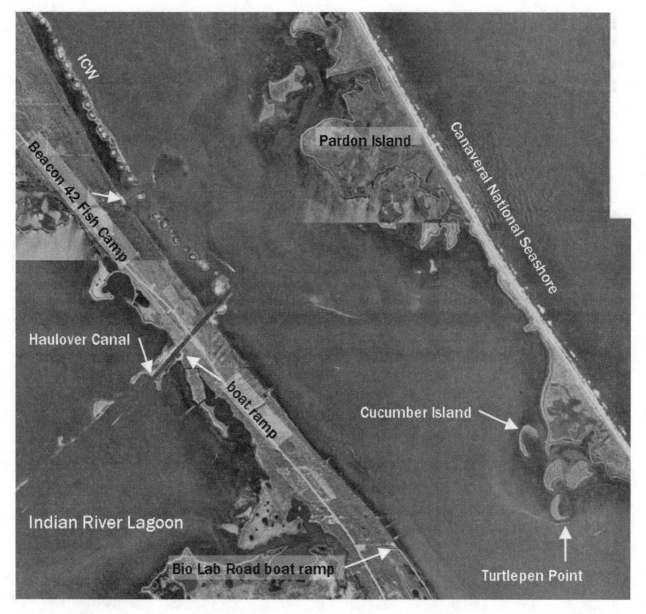

Haulover Canal connects the two lagoons in this stretch. The canal itself sometimes holds surprising numbers of fish- black drum, redfish, and trout. You never know what you might catch here though. I've gotten flounder, Spanish mackerel, and gag grouper in the canal.

Due east of the end of the canal is a shallow grassflat that runs along the shoreline. While poling here you can clearly hear the waves breaking on the beach that is only a few feet away.

All the flats on the east side of the lagoon hold fish sometimes. Navigation can be treacherous though, since none of the several bars that are here have any kind of markers on them. If you're new to the lagoon you'll stay out of trouble by staying on the west side.

Photo 5- Mosquito Lagoon, Cucumber Island to Max Hoeck Creek

NOTICE- Security Closure Update

Since the tragic events of September 11, 2001, most of this area has been closed to all boat traffic. The closure line runs from the dirt boat ramp at Bio Lab Road on the west side to the Observatory at parking lot 13 on the east side. If you go down here you may see other boats, quite a few of them. They are all out of compliance with the closure. The penalty for non-compliance is up to five years in prison and a fine of up to $50,000.

The most aggravating part about this closure is trying to find someone official to talk to who knows what they are talking about. The US Coast Guard at Port Canaveral (321.853.7601) and Kennedy Space Center Security (321.867.2121) should be able to give you an up to date report. Don't expect any one you talk to to know what's going on.

Overview

Some of the lagoon's best fishing opportunities lie in this section. Navigation can be treacherous due to many, mostly unmarked bars. But those same bars hold fish, frequently large specimens upwards of 20 pounds. At least if you hit a bar here you won't destroy your hull or lower unit. There aren't any rocks or other hard bottom.

The setup is much the same as the previous two areas- fairly straightforward along the western side, with bars, islands, sloughs, and other irregularities along the eastern side. Canaveral National Seashore's Playalinda Beach gives some access along the eastern side.

Max Hoeck Creek is the southern extremity of Mosquito Lagoon.

Access

On the western side is the National Wildlife Refuge dirt ramp at the old Atmospheric Testing Station (Bio Lab Road) as mentioned in the last section. Running south along the margin of the lagoon from this ramp is a dike road which gives small car-top boaters (canoeists and kayakers) and waders excellent access. During the winter months you can actually sightfish from your vehicle here.

On the eastern side there is a dirt ramp in the Playalinda Beach section of the National Seashore (fee required) at Eddy Creek. Adventurous canoeists, kayakers, and waders can also get into the lagoon from parking lot #12 at Playalinda Beach.

Fishing Here- West Side

The flat continues down the western side of lagoon from the boat ramp to the pilings at the remains of an old fish camp in the southwestern corner of the lagoon. The bottom is mostly manatee grass interspersed with white holes. Trout and redfish use this flat year round, and in the winter they will get into very shallow water if the weather is nice. That's why you can see them from your vehicle. Although it's a little soft you can wade this flat fairly easily.

As you get down into the area where the Middle Bank (the Whale Tail) is you may find

Due to security concerns, as of this writing most of the waters in this photo are closed to all vessels. When they will open again (if ever) is not known. The closed area includes everything south of a line between the dirt boat ramp at Bio Lab Road and the observatory on the east shoreline, south of Turtlepen Point.

The south end of the lagoon has excellent access for waders via the dike road that runs along the west side (and this road is still open). Canoes and kayaks are easily launched from several spots along this road.

On the east side, Eddy Creek has a dirt boat ramp. Folks using car-top boats can launch them at Parking Lot 12. Expect a short carry.

Flats that hold trout, reds, and black drum rim the basin here, and the Middle Bank (Whale Tail) often holds a school of big reds that could be found anywhere between its north side and Pelican Island. Again, the Middle Bank is not marked and is very hard to see unless the light is good. Lots of boaters run aground here.

a school of big reds that will sometimes use deeper sections of the westside flat.

Fishing Here- South End

For the purpose of this discussion we will consider the south end everything from the Middle Bank flat south. The Middle Bank (Whale Tail) is a triangular shaped flat more or less in the center of the lagoon. Its northern side runs east and west across the lagoon, and sometimes has a PVC pipe marking two northeast and northwest corners, but these are often absent, possibly pulled out by some of the fishing guides. Many people run aground here. There is a leaning section of four inch PVC pipe marking the southern point of the triangle. The water for a short distance on the south side of this leaning pipe is fairly deep and offers safe passage to all but the deepest draft boats. South of this is another flat known as the Middle Flat which extends most of the way from the leaning pipe to Pelican Island.

There is a large school of big redfish that love this area. They use all three sides of the Middle Bank, the Middle Flat, and sometimes the deeper sections of the westside flat. Like all schools of big reds in the lagoon, knowledge of their whereabouts spreads quickly when they show up, and they are heavily fished.

This entire area is also excellent for seatrout most of the year, offering shallow flats, edges, and deep water. Keep looking around and you're bound to find some.

Tarpon, usually less than 30 pounds, often like this area during some summers. Some years I see very thick concentrations of them in here. Other years none show up.

If you follow the eastern edge of the Middle Flat to the south, a slough will lead you past the eastern side of Pelican Island into Max Hoeck Creek. If you intend to run south of the end of this slough be advised there is no way out except by pushpole. It's very shallow back there. Legal sized redfish, and seatrout of all sizes, get back into this creek and around the south side of Pelican Island.

Directly to the south of the northeastern corner of the Middle Bank is a bar that extends out from Gallinipper Point. Although a pipe marks the western end of this bar a lot of people run aground on it. South of this bar a slough runs roughly to the southeast, onto a flat south of Gallinipper Point. This flat can be productive for both trout and reds.

Down in the very southeastern corner of the lagoon still another slough runs back into Eddy Creek. There is a boat ramp in here, and if nature calls you can tie up to the dock here and walk up to the chemical toilet that the National Seashore maintains. There is a deep hole back here by this dock that trout will collect in during cold weather. Redfish will also get into Eddy Creek sometimes.

Fishing Here- East Side

Inside (east of) and to the south of Cucumber Island the water is very shallow, but on higher water levels this area can be very productive. Cucumber Slough, a shallow slough surrounded by islands, likewise can fill up with reds and trout. High water levels are needed for this to happen.

The south end of the Cucumber Island flat ends at a long sandbar that runs in a NW/SE orientation from Turtlepen Point. I have always thought I should see a lot of fish here, but I hardly ever do. Manatees like it though- navigate with care.

East of Turtlepen Point there are more flats, and the south side of this flat is marked by a bar. Likewise I have never done very well here. Some other guides fish this area frequently, though, and I'm sure there's a reason for that.

There is a small island here near the shoreline, on the south side of which is a slough that runs almost all the way to the shoreline. On the southwest side of this slough, running north and south, is another bar. There is a structure on the shoreline that looks like an astronomical observatory that makes an excellent landmark. This bar is often very fishy, and sometimes has some very large fish around it- trout, reds, and black drum. If you're in the vicinity it's worth a few minutes to check.

The eastside flat from here south all the way to Gallinipper Point can be good, with both trout and reds. Getting up along this shoreline requires a commitment. Since it's so shallow for such a long distance it's a long pole back out again.

Photo 6- Indian River Lagoon - Turnbull Creek to Railroad Trestle

Overview

This is the northernmost extent of the Indian River Lagoon. Turnbull Creek rises in swamps to the north of US 1 and flows slowly south to empty into the Indian River Lagoon. In the Indian River Lagoon, the entire area north of the ICW is known as Turnbull Basin. The east side shoreline is in the Merritt Island National Wildlife Refuge (MINWR); the west, although largely undeveloped, is mostly in private ownership. MINWR boundary markers run up the middle of the lagoon all the way from the Dummit Cove area across the ICW and up to Turnbull Creek. A railroad track, frequently used by freight trains, runs along the west side, which mars the aesthetics somewhat.

The western shoreline also has a rather long slow speed zone, and the extreme north end of the river is also a slow speed manatee zone.

The eastern shoreline has points, coves, and creeks; the west side shoreline is almost perfectly regular, with a single exception- from the Praxair plant (large white building complex about a mile north of the railroad trestle) north for maybe two miles there is a dredged, navigable (by small boats) channel along the westside shoreline. The spoil was piled up to make small spoil islands on the eastern side of this channel. Speaking of spoil islands, a string of them follows the course of the ICW. Unlike the Mosquito Lagoon there are no bars (excepting spoil piles on the north side of the ICW). Navigation here is much easier.

For whatever reason there is generally less fishing pressure here than in the Mosquito Lagoon, and there are some large schools of very big redfish in here.

Access

-On the east side:

A dike road runs along the northeast side of the lagoon, from up near Turnbull Creek to the canals of an old, attempted but failed residential development. The north end of this road comes out on US 1, the south end on SR 3. The road gives waders and small boaters excellent access to this area.

Another dike road runs around Dummit Creek and part way around Dummit Cove. This road's north end is on SR 3 and the south end comes out on the Black Point Wildlife Drive.

There is an excellent if somewhat busy National Wildlife Refuge ramp at the Haulover Canal. There are no facilities, and there have been some problems with vehicle break-ins.

-On the west side:

There is a Brevard County ramp at the end of Huntington Avenue (off US 1) in Scottsmoor. The water is shallow and larger boats will definitely have a problem here.

There is a dirt ramp next to the Praxair plant, maintained by I have no idea whom. The water is fairly deep and skiffs shouldn't have any trouble using it.

Those with skiffs can also easily access this area from the excellent Brevard County facility at Parrish Park. There are restrooms and the Florida Fish and Wildlife Conservation Commission Division of Law Enforcement building is right next to it, so except for LeFils Fish Camp it's definitely the safest ramp in the entire area. It's hard to load your boat here when the wind is strong from the west.

Fishing Here- North End

The extreme north end of the Indian River Lagoon (north of the Scottsmoor boat ramp) is all posted slow speed manatee zone. It can be good for redfish and seatrout. Thick beds of manatee grass carpet the bottom. After heavy rains the water often gets too dark for sight fishing because of outflow from Turnbull Creek. Fish will get up into this creek itself sometimes, and it is navigable up to the US 1 bridge by small boats like Gheenoes and jonboats. It's a great place for hand powered craft.

During the summer and into the fall schools of jacks sometimes terrorize mullet here and I have also seen tarpon rolling here (small ones) during the summer, especially up by the mouth of Turnbull Creek. The islands at the mouth of the creek can shelter large numbers of redfish when the water is up high enough, and there's usually a lot of bait here. Schools of black drum will sometimes be found in the northeast corner of the river, accessible to waders from the dike road.

Waders can easily sightfish from this road during the winter months, at least until the Wildlife Refuge closes the road for duck season. Once it's been closed the road remains that way until one week after duck season ends, usually sometimes at the beginning of February. For up to date information on which roads are open when, call the Wildlife Refuge office at 321.861.0667.

Flats runs along the west side from Turnbull Creek all the way to the railroad trestle. While sometimes devoid of fish, when these flats are good they are awesome. Big schools of redfish get up here, sometimes fish in the 20 pounds and up range. Trout, tarpon, and jack crevalle are other visitors to the west side flat.

There is a school of big redfish that swim around in the deeper waters of the Turnbull Basin. Hard for the casual angler to locate, many guides have made their living from this school.

The dike road on the east shoreline here offers excellent access to the wader and those using hand powered boats. During the winter months you can sometimes see fish tailing from your vehicle here. The marsh ponds sometimes get fish in them, too. Fully exploring them necessitates a hand powered boat.

Fishing Here- East Side

The dike road takes a twisted path, following the irregular shoreline, all of which is accessible for waders until the end of the road. Pay particular attention to the culverts that drain the marsh, as fish will often collect at these when water is flowing from them.

At the point called the Hole in the Wall there is an old bombing target and a couple of islands, to the northeast of which is Griffis Bay. This entire area can be very productive for slot reds and seatrout, and if you look in deeper water all down this shoreline as far south as the Haulover Canal you may find a school of truly huge redfish. In order to locate these fish you need both good weather and a good dose of luck, since there isn't any particular structure on which they key.

Again, during the summer and fall big schools of crevalle will cruise along this shoreline. Sometimes they push a wake or are actually finned out, very easy to see. Other times showering mullet provide the clue.

The next very obvious structure on this shoreline is Duckroost Point. To the north is a cove that will hold fish sometimes. While it's fairly shallow, there is an old residential canal against the shoreline that will allow boaters to get out of there without a long pole.

To the south of Duckroost Point is Duckroost Cove, accessible to hand powered vessels launching at the north side of the Haulover Canal. Duckroost Cove can be barren for months, but it can also be very good. I have done quite well there on both reds and trout during the winter months. It's shallow and for those in skiffs there's no easy way out except by poling.

The Haulover Canal gets a lot of fishing pressure from anglers, much of which seems unjustified. Because I prefer to sightfish I don't often fish there, but I don't see many people catch much there other than catfish, toadfish, stingrays, and rocks. Having said that, schools of big reds come through, as do black drum (especially around the bridge fenders). Actually every species of fish that's found in this section of the Indian River Lagoon has to pass through the canal if they wish to pass from the Indian River Lagoon to the Mosquito Lagoon.

South of the Haulover Canal the shoreline continues southeast for a short distance, then turns at Dummit Creek and heads roughly west, then at Black Point it turns and heads south.

At the start of this stretch is a small island called Granny Island. Flats to the east, west, and south of this island can all be excellent for both reds and trout, as can Dummit Cove and Dummit Creek. Watch out for manatees in this area. Big white sand patches on the bottom here sometimes fill up with fish. Since the water is usually clean here these white spots make the area a sight fisher's dream, as the fish are very easy to see.

Heading towards Black Point, the shoreline along Marsh Bay is all white sand flats with patches of grass. During the winter this white sand loads up with big trout that like to sun themselves. These are some of the spookiest fish you'll ever find, very hard to catch. On the bright side the bottom here is firm and excellent for wading. Redfish also use this shoreline.

Black Point itself, and the shoreline south all the way to the railroad trestle, is much the same. When it's good it can be wonderful, but sadly this area isn't very consistent. It can remain barren for extended periods of time.

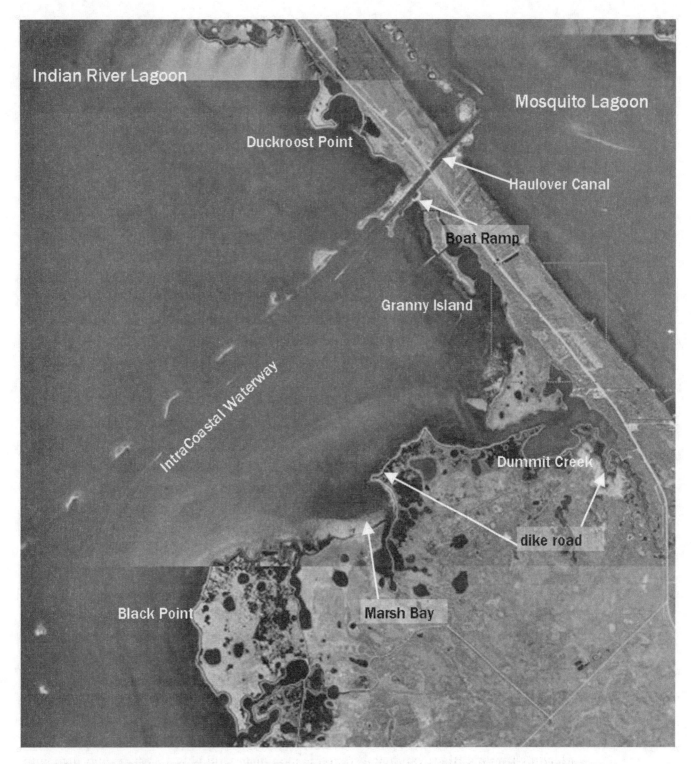

The flats here between the Haulover Canal and Black Point can be very productive for trout and redfish. A dike road runs around Dummit Creek on its south side, giving the wader and small boater excellent access. Some of the dike roads (including this one) are closed during waterfowl hunting season, so call the Merritt Island Wildlife Refuge at 321.861.0667 for a status report before driving over here.

The railroad track leading to the trestle is built on a causeway. There are a lot of manatees that use this area, so be careful. The causeway itself is a large piece of structure, and as you might guess it often holds fish. On the northeast side a creek empties into the Indian River and this place holds redfish reasonably consistently. Along this side of the causeway reds and trout both use the white sand bottom, along which you can both pole and wade.

Fishing Here- The Spoil Islands

Running along the middle of the Indian River through this stretch is the ICW channel, which was dredged to its depth of 12 feet. The dredge spoil was piled up along the channel in discreet locations, making a string of islands. These islands provide structure in relatively deep water, so as you can probably guess, they sometimes hold fish.

Topwater plugs at dawn may be the most exciting way to fish these islands. Look for schools of mullet and work the bait around them. Later in the day jigs can score, and bait can work anytime. I often see folks pulled up on the island itself still fishing, and conversations with these people indicate that sometimes they do quite well, especially on seatrout.

Fishing Here- West Side

As described in the overview, this shoreline is very regular and runs generally north and south. A flat runs from the shoreline out about 150 yards, and then drops off into deeper water. Large (20 pounds plus) redfish can be found anywhere along this edge, from the boat ramp at Scottsmoor all the way south to the railroad trestle. Although sometimes they will be singles, they are usually found in fairly large schools containing 100 or more fish. They have been known to get up onto the flat.

You may also find slot sized reds (legal fish, between 18 and 27 inches) here, both in schools and as singles. Trout also use this flat along its entire length. In the summer and into the fall schools of jacks will terrorize mullet along along this flat, and they particularly like the corner by the railroad trestle.

From Scottsmoor south for about two miles the entire flat is a posted slow speed safety zone. Travel on this section is by idle speed, electric motor, or poling only.

About a mile north of the railroad trestle is a large white building complex, which is the Praxair plant, a company that sells compressed gas. Just to the north of their property is a dirt boat ramp. Running north along the shoreline from this ramp for about three miles in a dredged channel, navigable by small boats up to where it dead ends. Manatees use this channel frequently- navigate with caution. Small tarpon get in here during the summer, and it's a well known cold weather trout spot. The spoil was piled on the river side, making a series of small islands, which sometimes hold slot sized redfish singles. The culverts along this stretch of shoreline are obvious fish attractors.

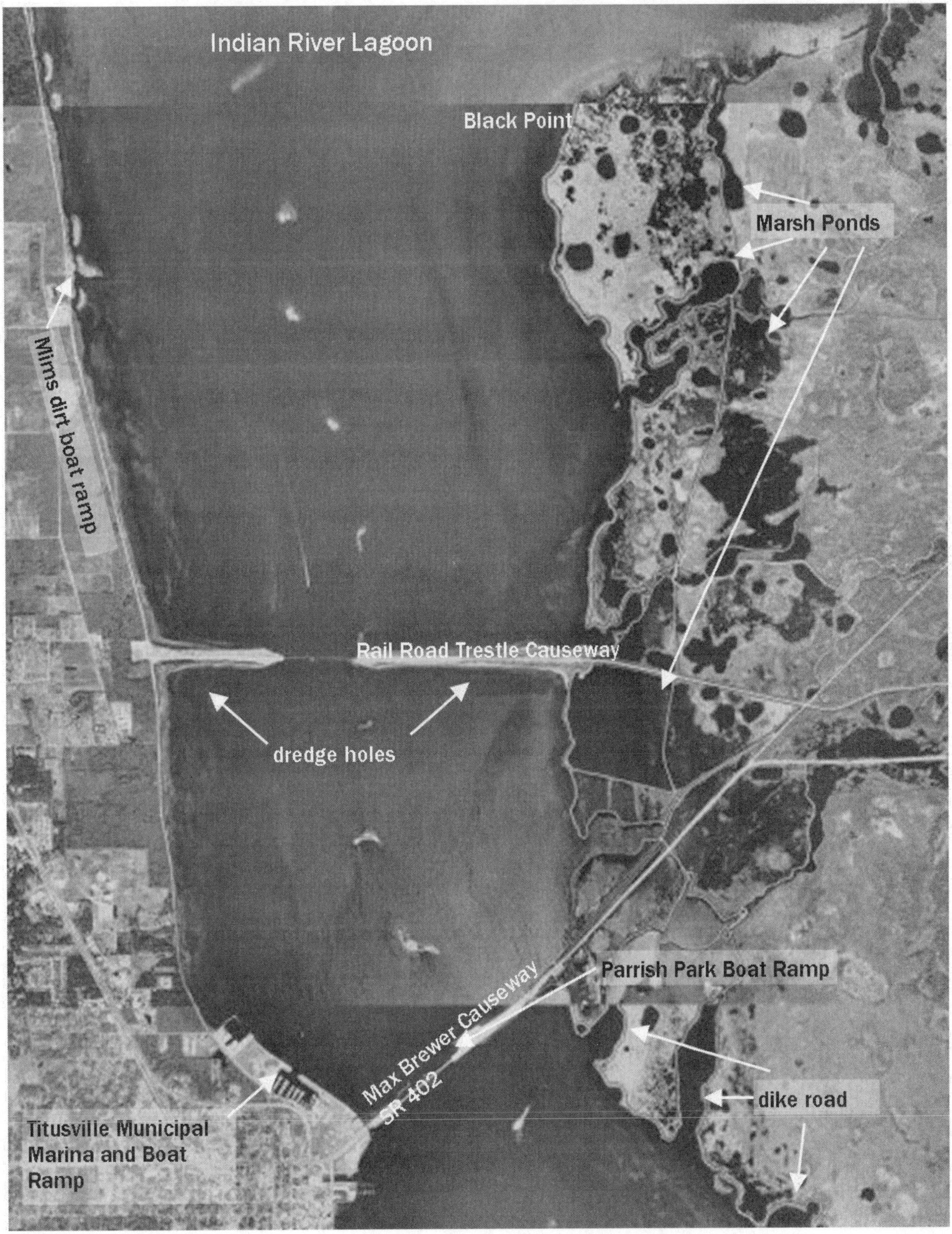

Indian River Lagoon

Black Point

Marsh Ponds

Mims dirt boat ramp

Rail Road Trestle Causeway

dredge holes

Parrish Park Boat Ramp

Max Brewer Causeway
SR 402

dike road

Titusville Municipal
Marina and Boat
Ramp

Photo 7 Indian River Lagoon- Railroad Trestle to Morse Creek

Overview

In this stretch of the Indian River Lagoon the eastern shoreline is mostly Merritt Island National Wildlife Refuge or NASA property. It's a great place from which to watch rocket launches! Several creeks and coves indent this shoreline, and a dike road runs along the shoreline from SR 405 south to Peacock Pocket. This road provides excellent access for shore fishermen, waders, and car-top boaters. The bottom is carpeted with manatee grass and the water tends to be clean. Wading along here is good to excellent due to the firm bottom. Much of the shoreline through here lies in a slow speed manatee zone.

Some spoil islands line the east side of the ICW out in the middle of the river. Many are below the water's surface most of the time.

Along the western side runs US 1, and the city of Titusville. The shoreline is quite developed, with lots of docks and seawalls. The water tends to be murky because of the rainwater runoff and lack of grass on the bottom. Docks and seawalls are structure, so fish still use this shoreline. The entire river west of the ICW channel from the railroad trestle south to and beyond the NASA Causeway is a slow speed manatee zone.

Access

-East side

On the northeastern side of the SR 405 bridge is the Brevard County facility at Parrish Park, one of the best ramps on the entire Space Coast. Rest rooms (not open until 8:00 AM, unfortunately) and pavilions are provided, and this parking lot is adjacent to the Fish and Wildlife Conservation Commission station, making it one of the safest ramps you can use. This ramp gets very nasty with a hard west wind.

-West side

Just north of the Titusville Municipal Marina is a City of Titusville dirt ramp. Although not as nice as the ramp at Parrish Park, this ramp is protected by a seawall and is sheltered in any kind of weather. It's quite shallow, but can be easily used by smaller sized fishing skiffs.

Just south of the intersection of US 1 and SR 50 is the Brevard County facility at Kennedy Point Park. From the water the Kennedy Point Marina provides an excellent landmark. Another excellent facility, it's protected by a breakwater, making it attractive in any weather.

Fishing Here- East Side

On the southeast side of the railroad trestle is one of the dredge holes from which the material to build the causeway was drawn. This hole sometimes holds big tarpon in the summer, but you need to be there early in the morning to see them rolling. The same hole will hold trout during cold weather.

Along the extreme eastern end of the causeway, in the corner, and south down the

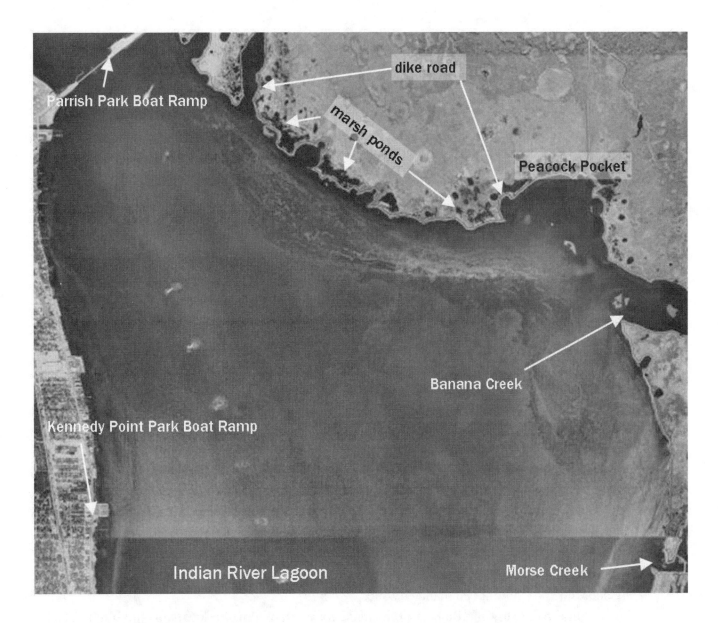

The dike road along the northeast side of this photo gives great access to waders and small boaters. Beautiful and sometimes very productive grassflats run along the entire east side of the lagoon here. In front of Banana Creek and Morse Creek are particularly good places to try. Be advised that much of this shoreline lies inside of a manatee slow speed zone. Entry into both Banana Creek and Morse Creek is prohibited.

Along the west side, seawalls and docks provide a lot of structure for fish. This side is relatively lightly fished, and could be a bonanza for the angler more concerned with fish than aesthetics.

shoreline to the creek mouth redfish and trout can sometimes be found. It's a good place to look when winter winds come out of the north or northwest.

Along both sides of the SR 405 Causeway (Max Brewer Causeway) east of the ICW is an unofficial watersports area for wind surfers and personal water craft. It is strongly suggested that you avoid fishing here.

As you continue south down the east shoreline you come to several creeks. Gator Creek is the first, Catfish Creek the second. Dike roads surround these creeks giving superb access. Particularly in late winter and early spring these creeks can load up with fish, both reds and trout. Waders using surface lures can have tremendous fishing at this time of year. For some reason I have never seen many fish on the flats right here, but as you get down by Peacock Pocket the flats can hold large numbers of seatrout, redfish, and jack crevalle. Again, these flats are quite firm, making for some excellent wading.

Peacock Pocket itself has a softer bottom, but can also be full of redfish and trout. The road that provides access here runs directly off of SR 405, and the easy access and relatively consistent action make this one of my favorite wading spots. The farther south you wade off the dike road the firmer the bottom becomes, and once you get out to the numerous white spots out near the edge of the flat you are in definite big redfish territory. Sadly, since Sept. 11, 2001 this road has been closed for security reasons, but you can still drive back here by taking the long way along the dike road.

This water is more easily accessed by boat. This entire area, including Peacock Pocket and the mouth of Banana Creek, is fairly consistent for both trout and reds and big redfish are always a distinct possibility. Banana Creek is closed to all entry, so it provides a safe haven for our finned friends. Particularly during the mullet run in September and October crevalle action can be explosive. You may also find small tarpon or an occasional snook at this time of year.

Also, as you motor into this section, look for the day markers running north and south in a line roughly from Peacock Pocket south the NASA Causeway. From these signs east, this entire shoreline is a slow speed manatee zone.

On the flat between Banana Creek and Morse Creek (known locally as the VAB flat) the bottom has big white patches that sometimes hold large numbers of fish. Reds can be in singles, small groups, or large schools. When the water is high they will get right along the shoreline and can be seen and heard from a distance, blasting minnows. Again, the bottom is hard here and wading is very pleasant.

Just north of Morse Creek is a culvert that is one of my favorites, since when the water is up and the culvert is running there are almost always fish here. You could get trout, reds, ladyfish, tarpon, and snook all at this one small spot.

Morse Creek itself often holds snook, reds, and trout, and jacks, ladyfish, and small tarpon are not infrequent visitors. The creek entrance is at least a foot deeper than the surrounding flat, making it an important piece of structure in this area.

The VAB (Vehicle Assembly Building, the largest building in Florida) flat extends out from the shoreline about a half mile. At the outside edge is a frequently poorly defined bar, but it is particularly noticeable due west of Morse Creek. This bar will sometimes hold fish, and like all bars that will hold fish and are adjacent to deep water, big fish are sometimes found.

Fishing Here- The Spoil Islands

I don't spend much time working these islands, although I imagine trout lurk around them much of the time. In the late summer/early fall, when the bait begins its migration, schools of jacks, ladyfish, trout, and bluefish will crash schools of glass minnows out along the ICW on both sides of the channel, especially around the spoil islands. Look for flocks of terns and gulls diving to locate this very exciting action.

Fishing Here- West Side

On the southwest side of the railroad trestle is one of the dredge holes from which the material to build the causeway was drawn. This hole sometimes holds big tarpon in the summer, but you need to be there early in the morning to see them rolling. The same hole will hold trout during cold weather.

Along the extreme western end of the causeway, in the corner, and south down the shoreline to the stone jetty at the boat builders, redfish and trout can sometimes be found. It's a good place to look when winter winds come out of the north or northwest. Since it's all in a manatee zone it's more lightly fished than some other places.

The stone jetty surrounds a small and fairly deep turning basin that sometimes holds trout during cold weather.

The Titusville Municipal Marina likewise has a fairly deep turning basin that sometimes holds trout during cold weather.

On the northwest side of the Max Brewer Causeway is the Titusville Municipal Pier. It's a good place to drown shrimp. Once in a while people actually catch a fish or two there.

South of the Max Brewer Causeway down to the Holiday Inn it's all urban fishing, which I don't like to do. I don't fish this stretch, preferring the undeveloped shorelines nearby. However, the fish don't share my prejudice. There are lots of docks and seawalls that fish like to use as hideouts. If you do some searching in here you can probably find a couple of good spots that aren't heavily fished.

When I've spoken to anglers who fish the professional redfish tour, a lot of them like this shoreline. They do well here casting jigs around the many docks and seawalls.

Photo 8 Indian River Lagoon- Morse Creek to SR 528

Overview

Although the lagoon is fairly featureless in this stretch, it can offer some good fishing. Major landscape features include the NASA Causeway, the Rinker Canal on the east side, the two power stations of the west side, the Canaveral Barge Canal, and the SR 528 causeway.

Both the east side of the lagoon down to the Rinker Canal and the west side for about a mile north and south of the NASA Causeway are mostly undeveloped. US 1 runs along the west side of the lagoon, so there are many residences and condos along this shoreline south of the point just described. There are also homes along the east side between the Rinker Canal and the Barge Canal. Many of the homes on both sides of the lagoon have docks, many of which hold fish. In general, old dilapidated docks fish better than new ones. Avoid docks that have bait buckets tied off on them.

The power stations can also be enormous fish magnets. See West Side below.

This entire section of the Indian River Lagoon from the Max Brewer Causeway south to the SR 528 Causeway is a manatee slow speed zone west of the ICW.

Access

-West side only

The Kennedy Point Park boat ramp is on US 1, just south of SR 50.

In Port St. John there is a paved boat ramp on US 1 just north of the south power station. This ramp is nasty when there's a hard northeast or east wind.

Stopping for any reason along the NASA Causeway is strictly prohibited.

Fishing Here- East Side

From Morse Creek south to the NASA Causeway the shoreline frequently holds redfish, usually in singles or small groups but sometimes in good sized schools. Trout are also fairly common. Again, during the summer and fall crevalle can be thick.

The northeast side of the NASA Causeway (accessible only by boat) can be an exceptionally fishy place. The causeway was filled with spoil from a dredge hole located here. This hole can hold large numbers of trout during cold snaps. Since the hole is over 10 feet deep, it also provides haven for a school of large redfish that patrol this area, all the way out to where the bridge starts. I have seen large trout, snook, and tarpon cruising this edge, and sometimes in the winter a school of black drum will get up in here.

A lot of manatees use this area, which is as already mentioned a slow speed zone.

The southeast side of the causeway can likewise be quite fishy, although there's no dredge hole there. But trout, reds, snook, and sometimes black drum all use this side of the causeway, especially during the winter months. Additionally, it's frequently a good place to look for large redfish.

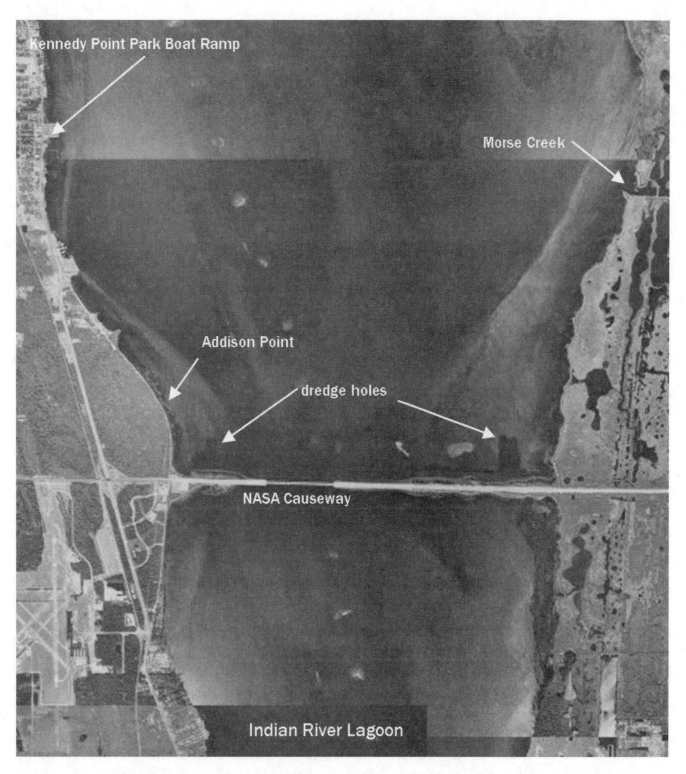

On either side of the NASA Causeway, fish use the flats on both sides of the lagoon, although the water tends to be cleaner on the east side. The causeway itself, and the dredge holes on its north side, often holds fish. Vertical jigging under this bridge is frequently productive.

Motorists may not stop on this causeway for any reason.

Along this entire shoreline south to the Rinker Canal redfish and trout can frequently be found, and jacks like this area during their summer and fall rampages. In deeper water in this section a school of large reds sometimes works. The sea of stakes you will see in still deeper water mark clam leases. And best of all, once you get out away from the causeway you are no longer in a manatee zone.

The Rinker Canal goes nowhere, and it is a manatee zone. But its 10 foot depths offer a haven to trout, reds, snook, and tarpon. The trout like it when it's cold outside, since it supplies them with a thermal refuge. Cast jigs into the deeper water and work them slowly. The snook and redfish are there spring through fall. Work the shoreline with weedless jigs. Tarpon are there all summer long, way up in the back at the cul de sac. Look and you'll see them rolling.

South of the Rinker Canal are still more flats used by trout, reds, and jacks, but now there are residential docks, too. The water under the docks in this area tends to be rather shallow, so they hold fish infrequently. But when the water level comes up, trout, reds, and snook will all use them.

As you head south you will come to a residential canal, beyond which are a pair of islands (Pine Island) that run out from the shoreline. The little stretch of flat between these two features often holds good numbers of redfish.

I have always thought that the area around Pine Island should hold fish, but I have never seen any there. I know that fish do get around the residential canals that are on the shoreline between Pine Island and the Barge Canal, but I seldom fish this piece of the river. Neither do I fish the spoil islands just to the north of the Barge Canal. But trout and reds use this entire area.

Fishing Here- West Side

Heading south from Kennedy Point Park you will see a significant point of land come off the west shoreline, south of which the shoreline is undeveloped to the NASA Causeway. This stretch can be very good for both trout and reds, and comparatively few people fish it. The deeper water in here can get big schools of mixed jacks, trout, ladyfish, and bluefish crashing glass minnows during the fall bait migration.

There is a dredge hole on this side of the causeway, but it doesn't seem to hold fish nearly as well as the east side does.

Similarly, while the southwest side of the causeway will sometimes hold fish, it doesn't seem nearly as consistent as the east side.

South of the causeway residential docks start to appear and continue to the north power station. These docks will hold fish- trout and reds all year, snook and tarpon during the summer.

The outflow of north power station sometimes attracts incredible numbers of fish, including jacks, ladyfish, tarpon, snook, snapper, sheepshead, and more. When it's good it's a fish every cast, no matter what you throw. For several years the all tackle world record ladyfish was a five pound fish taken at this spot. Although it's generally best during the winter months, be advised that as of this writing the area inside the buoys is closed to all entry between November 15 and March 31 in the name of manatee protection.

Homes with residential docks line almost the entire west shoreline of the Indian River Lagoon here. These docks provide shelter for snook, tarpon, redfish, and seatrout. Sheepshead, snapper, black drum, and spadefish are also seen around these docks sometimes.

The power plant outflows are fish magnets during the winter months. Unfortunately the federal government has closed these areas to all entry during the winter months in the name of manatee protection.

On the east side, the shoreline north of the RInker Canal is undeveloped and sometimes holds large numbers of trout, redfish, and crevalle. Big schools of redfish are sometimes seen in here.

The Rinker Canal will hold snook, redfish, seatrout, and tarpon, depending on the season. Lots of manatees use this canal.

South of the Rinker Canal some homes have docks on the river, which can be productive at higher water levels. While I know some people who do well here, south of Pine Island has never been very good to me.

The berms protecting the fuel barge canal will sometimes hold fish, especially snook, when the water level is up. Tarpon sometimes get in the access channel in the summertime. They can be real big ones.

South of these berms a condo has a seawall that lines the river almost all the way to the Port St. John boat ramp. The sand bottom by this wall sometimes holds trout during the winter months, when they gather there to sun themselves.

The outflows of the south power station, like that of the north station, sometimes attract incredible numbers of fish, including jacks, ladyfish, tarpon, snook, snapper, sheepshead, sharks, and more. Although it's generally best during the winter months, be advised that as of this writing the area inside the buoys is closed to all entry between November 15 and March 31 in the name of manatee protection.

The berm on the south side of the outflows usually holds snook all summer long. The water near the end is deep and offers good protection to the fish. I've also seen good numbers of redfish, jacks, and ladyfish out here. Lots of manatees use this area.

The shoreline south of the power station all the way to SR 528 is developed with homes. Lots of residential docks are found here, and those docks shelter snook, redfish, trout, and tarpon. This section of the river is relatively lightly fished and deserves some exploration by any angler more interested in fish than aesthetics.

Photo 9- Banana River Lagoon, NASA Causeway to SR 528 (the No Motor Zone)

NOTICE- Security Closures

Due to security concerns raised since September 11, 2001, the entire east side of the section described below has been closed to all entry. The closed area contains all the water between the power line just north of SR 528 and the NASA Causeway, east of the marked channel running north and south. The penalty for ignoring this closure can be as high as a $50,000 fine and/or five years in prison. When the area will open again is not known as of this writing. Trespassing in the closed area is a Federal offense.

Overview

This piece of water may have the best fishing in the entire Indian River Lagoon system. No motors of any kind are allowed in most of this area, so the fish are not constantly run over by boats with combustion engines. That gives the angling experience here an aesthetic that's only available in a few other places in the entire state. If you fish here during the week you may not see another boat all day.

Many different kinds of vessels are used by enterprising anglers to access this section. I

NASA Security Zone

NASA Causeway

Banana River Lagoon

Buck Creek
(restricted area)

Duck Point

Cactus Point

Middle Point

Home Point

KARS Park

marked channel

canoe launches

Cape Canaveral Air Force Station

Port Canaveral

use a canoe or a kayak, but I also see rowboats, sailboats, peddleboats, and even saw a Zodiak being poled up in here one time.

Keep in mind if you're considering fishing here that if a south wind comes up you'll have to travel against it to get out. Usually, I don't pay that much attention to the weather forecast since it is so frequently wrong, but if a south or southeast wind is forecast when I'm thinking of coming here I always decide to go elsewhere. I don't enjoy it when my day's fishing turns into a survival test, and that can happen very easily here.

Fish species found here include the usual redfish (but to impressive sizes), seatrout, snook, tarpon, jacks, and black drum. The largest tailing fish you will ever throw to are the huge black drum that live here. Although bait (clams, shrimp, or crabs) is the best way to catch them, they take artificials and even flies surprisingly well.

Like other nearby bodies of water, the eastern shoreline has creeks, points, and coves while the west side is straight and relatively featureless. But neither fishes better than the other over an extended period of time.

The eastern shoreline is Canaveral Air Force Station property. The western shoreline is NASA property. Neither of those agencies want you on their land, so stay in the water or you may be visited by rather upset security personnel. In my experience these people have very little sense of humor, and they take their jobs very seriously. Also, this area closes three days prior to a shuttle launch. Don't go up there then or you will definitely be visited by security personnel.

Remember that fishing is fishing. Like anywhere else, you can have fishless days here.

Access

A handful of lucky folks that work for NASA or the Air Force station can get access up in KARS Park, from the air force station, or even sometimes from the NASA Causeway (!). If you are retired military and have your military I.D. you can get access through KARS Park. For the rest of us...

-East side. From the north side of SR 401 (across from the Port Canaveral cruise terminals) before you reach the gate of the Canaveral Air Force Station there are several pull-offs where you can launch a small boat. After you pass under the power lines you are in the no motor zone.

-West side. The north end of Banana River Drive dead-ends at the Canaveral Barge Canal. Small boats can be launched here. Travel north up the shoreline until you reach KARS Park. You will see the day boards marking the no motor zone. Once you pass those signs you're in!

Fishing Here- East Side

Every inch of the shoreline from SR 401 up to the spoil islands can and does sometimes hold fish. Redfish and trout can be found here at any time. Snook are common during the summer and fall (until about the end of October). Small tarpon will often be found in here in good numbers some summers. While you might find the black drum on any day, you don't expect to see them except during the colder months, from about Thanksgiving until Easter.

Heading north up the shoreline the first real landmark you come to is a stand of Australian pines, on the north side of which a creek empties. Fish of all kinds can be found here.

Continuing north the next major landmark is a big telephone pole (no wires) sticking out of about a foot of water. Another creek empties in here. Yes, fish of all kinds can be found here.

Still moving north, a large point called Home Point extends out into the Banana River Lagoon. On the south side of this a little bay (Duck Pond) goes back up into that piece of land. This can be an excellent spot. On the northeast side of this bay a small dredge hole can load up with snook, trout, redfish, and tarpon. A stealthy approach is mandatory. If the water level is up this entire bay can be full of fish.

North of this point is a small cove that has been very good to me over the years for reds, snook and black drum. Look into deeper water to see larger fish.

On the north side of this cove is yet another point (Middle Point), followed by another cove. Likewise, this is a very good place, with large number of big reds and black drum tailing in here during the winter sometimes. Slot sized fish will be found working along the shoreline.

The next point is known as Cactus Point. Between Cactus Point and the spoil islands is Quartermain Cove, another excellent area. A creek drains into this cove, and this creek can just load up with fish. This creek mouth is small, so you have to be the first visitor of the day if you want to have success here. Big trout love this place during cold weather.

The spoil islands should perhaps be called the Spoiling Islands, since a trip here may spoil you for anything but Alaska. Lots of big fish use these islands, and big tailers can be found here during the winter, both red and black drum. It is a long paddle from SR 401.

North of the spoil islands I've never been. I've never seen the need, and I believe there's a restricted area up here by where they keep the solid rocket booster recovery vessels.

We need to back up now. Still on the east side, but out off the shore close to a mile or so, runs a series of bars. The first one lies 1.2 miles north of SR 401, out in front of the Australian pine grove. This bar holds fish, and sometimes big fish, both reds and black drum. Trout use this bar too. Actually this statement holds true for every bar, all the way up to the spoil islands. If you want big fish, these bars are the place to look.

Fishing Here- West Side

Once the boat is launched at the barge canal you have to cross the canal and head north up the shoreline. This flat can immediately be productive for reds, snook, trout, small tarpon, and jacks, and there have been days when I never got near the no motor zone and didn't regret it at all. The first really big redfish I ever caught was right under the power line here, and the cover photograph of Flyfishing for Redfish was shot here as well.

I'm often asked about the no motor zone, "How far do you have to go?" That depends on the fish, and I never go any farther than necessary to find them. If they're on the first flat I hit, so much the better. In my experience it's hard to catch fish when you're holding a paddle.

That having been said, when you get to KARS Park there's a dredged channel that comes off the boat ramp here. This channel sometimes holds fish of course- trout, reds, and snook. Look for signs of activity.

After crossing the channel you're in the NMZ proper. The edge of the flat curves off towards the northeast, clearly visible when the water is low. I have seen some nice schools of fish right here, as well as some big singles. But usually you need to keep heading north.

The first major landmark is a large building with big dish antennae all over it. Before you get there you will see a telephone line running along the bank. This shoreline can be quite productive, and during some summers large numbers of tarpon in the 20 pound range will be in a little trough out 100 feet or so off the shoreline.

Following the shoreline north, the next major landmark is a tall radio tower another mile or so past the first building. Before you get there you will pass a small point called Duck Point, to the northwest of which is a small, shallow slough. This entire area can be very productive for redfish, and sometimes black drum (colder months) and snook (warmer months) will be found.

By the tower itself a creek enters the river. Again, this is a reasonably consistent redfish area. Snook can also be found here during warmer months.

Reds will be found the entire way north up the shoreline as far as and past the bar marked by a number of white PVC pipes. I'll have more to say about this bar in a bit.

Past the bar the shoreline continues productive past the mouth of Buck Creek, all the way to the NASA causeway. Do not go into Buck Creek, as it's a restricted area.

Now back to the bar, the Buck Creek Basin, and the bombing target. Unlike the bars on the east side, which run parallel to the shoreline, this one runs out from the shore at a right angle. On the south side of the bar slightly deeper water attracts and holds big reds and black drum during the cooler months. This entire area is an excellent place to look for these large fish. The end of the bar can hold trout at any time, snook during the summer, and reds and black drum during the winter. If the water is up high enough they will get right on top of the bar.

North of the bar, in a triangle between it, the bombing target, and the mouth of Buck Creek, is a slightly deeper basin which can hold large numbers of big fish of all kinds. I have seen snook, tarpon, big reds, and jacks here during the summer months and big reds and black drum during the winter. If you make it up this far it's an excellent place to check.

The outer edge of the west side flat from the channel at KARS Park all the way to the NASA Causeway consists mostly of a firm (good to wade) white sand bar. It's hard to find if the water is up, but at lower water levels some time should be spent looking out here if the weather allows it. Like many bars adjacent to deeper water this one can hold large specimens of both redfish and black drum. Trout and snook will both lay up on top of it.

The NASA Causeway itself is a large piece of structure that many fish will relate to. If you made it up this far you should examine it carefully.

There is a bridge over the river at the NASA causeway. Do not go under the bridge. All waters to the north are strictly no entry.

Photo 10- Banana River Lagoon- SR 528 to Horti Point (includes Port Canaveral)

Overview

This section of the Banana River Lagoon has heavily developed shorelines with many residential docks and canals. It also has a lot of water that is slow speed manatee zone, (both sides of the lagoon between SR 528 and SR 520, marked by dayboards, and the east side of the lagoon south of SR 520, also marked with dayboards) so you can't make a quick run anywhere along the east shoreline. It's illegal in many places on the west side as well.

SR 528 crosses the lagoon on a causeway at the north end of this section. SR 520 crosses the lagoon on a large causeway about midway through this section.

South of SR 520 a long peninsula comes down the west shoreline of the lagoon, ending at Horti Point. To the west of this peninsula is Newfound Harbor, which narrows to Sykes Creek at its northern end. Sykes Creek runs back up into the Canaveral Barge Canal.

On the southeast side of this section lies the 1000 Islands area. This maze of residential canals and islands offers an excellent place to fish even during the worst weather.

Access

-West Side- there is an excellent boat ramp at Kelly Park, a Brevard County facility complete with playground, restrooms, and pavilions, located on Banana River Drive, just south of SR 528. There is also a paved ramp at Kiwanis Park, maintained by the city of Cocoa. This park is on the north side of SR 520 on the east side of Sykes Creek.

-East side- there is a paved ramp on the southeast side of the SR 520 causeway, almost across the street from the hospital.

There is an excellent, if somewhat hard to find, ramp at Ramp Road in Cocoa Beach, in the 1000 Islands area.

Fishing Here- East Side

Running north and south just south of the SR 528 causeway, well out off the shoreline, is a long sandbar, the north end of which is clearly marked by an old bombing target. Reds and trout use this bar frequently, and jacks will pin bait against it when they get in the lagoon.

A string of pipes mark an east-west channel that leads through the bar, allowing access to the east shoreline. This shoreline was largely created with fill that was dredged out of the lagoon, so there's a large dredge hole which holds trout when it gets cold, and manatees almost all the time. The shoreline is very regular and runs almost north and south until it makes a 90 degree turn to the east. Then it turns to the south again, and has been less altered in this section. Lots of docks hold fish sometimes- trout , reds, snook, and tarpon, all the way south to the SR 528 causeway. The canals just north of the causeway will hold trout in the wintertime.

Like many causeways, this one will hold fish. The area around the Canaveral Hospital in particular can be productive.

The causeway is a lot less productive on the south side, perhaps because of the boat ramp that's there. The ramp is on a dredged channel to the south of which is a flat. The west side of this flat is marked by a sand bar that runs generally north and south. Schools of large redfish can sometimes be found on either side of this bar, as can schools of smaller reds, trout, and jacks. All this area is in a slow speed manatee zone.

Along the east shoreline is a dredged channel which leads into the canal system of the 1000 Islands. These canals hold at various times of the year trout, jacks, ladyfish, snook, and tarpon. The canals can be fished in almost any weather. A trolling motor is a huge help here. As a matter of fact, effectively fishing these canals without a trolling motor is almost impossible.

The Houseboat Cut on the south side of this flat is a dredged channel which no longer being maintained and is silting in. Islands on both sides of it often hold redfish. The flat to the south is a good spot to cast for seatrout.

Just south of this is a peninsula on which sits the golf course. On the south side of the golf course a dredged channel runs east and west. It will take you back into the canals north of Ramp Road. These canals hold trout, snook, and tarpon, and sometimes redfish.

South of the golf course on the far side of the channel is another flat which holds redfish. When the water is up the shoreline will hold reds, trout, and snook. At the south end of these islands, where the island shoreline curves back toward the east, is a large flat well known for producing big redfish.

As we continue south we pass the south channel coming out from the boat ramp at Ramp Road. The coves and canals here are a good winter seatrout area.

The shoreline between here and Patrick AFB is residential in character with a lot of docks. Some of these docks hold fish. But generally there are better places to fish, even on this shoreline. Down by the Patrick AFB runways there is a dredged channel right along the shoreline, clearly marked by the tangle of dead trees on the west side of it. This area is frequently productive for seatrout, redfish, and snook, as far south as the end of the trees. The shoreline between these trees and the Pineda Causeway is usually barren.

The power lines that run parallel to the shoreline here offer some structure to an otherwise featureless area. Consequently they will hold fish sometimes, including black drum. The Pineda Causeway itself will often hold drum during the winter months.

Fishing Here- West Side

Between the SR 528 causeway and the SR 520 causeway the entire west shore is a slow speed manatee zone, except for the east-west channels that access the residential canals along this shoreline. These channels give the angler reasonably easy access to these flats and the canals, all of which hold fish- trout, reds, tarpon (summertime) and snook (also summertime). There's a lot of deep water here which provides a thermal refuge for fish during cold snaps, making it a good winter spot. The canals are short, but there are so many of them that even in

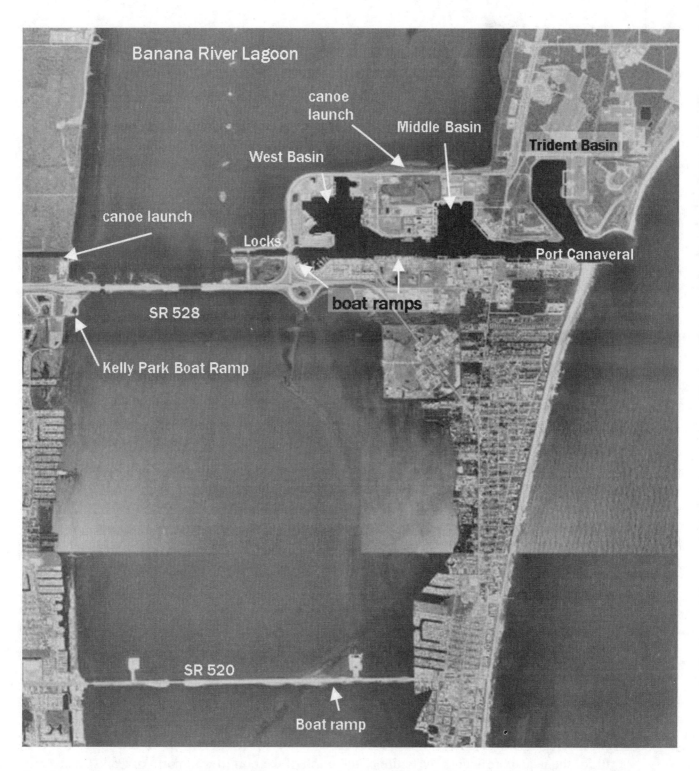

Banana River Lagoon

canoe launch

West Basin

Middle Basin

Trident Basin

canoe launch

Locks

Port Canaveral

boat ramps

SR 528

Kelly Park Boat Ramp

SR 520

Boat ramp

Port Canaveral offers fish a deep water habitat not otherwise available to them. The list of fish species who come into the port itself is fairly long, and includes sheepshead, mangrove snapper, snook, ribbonfish, flounder, jack crevalle, ladyfish, moon-fish, and more. Security concerns since September 11, 2001 make fishing around vessels and docks in the port much more difficult- security boats chase you off, or arrest you if you don't take the hint. I always take the hint when someone with an automatic weapon tells me to move.

Canals and docks on both sides of the Banana River here will hold fish.

windy weather you can spend an entire day here exploring.

The shoreline between SR 520 and Horti Point has never produced any fish of any kind for me. I don't see why fish, especially trout, wouldn't use this area, but I've never found it to be productive. Perhaps I need to check here more often.

Horti Point itself does sometimes hold reds, trout, and snook around the islands that are there. This is a good place to wade. As you go up the east side of Newfound Harbor up to SR 520 the residential docks will hold fish including reds, trout, and snook.

Heading south along the shoreline on the west side of Newfound Harbor are shallow grassflats which often hold reds and trout and sometimes hold large schools of reds, both slot sized and the big ones. All docks in this section should be worked carefully. Sometimes they will also hold mangrove snapper. Tarpon and snook sometimes hold on this flat during the summer months as well. Also, manatees are frequently found in this area, so navigate with caution. At the time I'm writing this the area is not a manatee zone, but it soon will be.

Continuing south out of Newfound Harbor you will encounter signs along the west side of the Banana River Lagoon which mark a large, slow speed manatee zone. The two islands on the east end of this line of signs are often a good place to look for both reds and trout. Try to stay upwind, as the islands are bird rookeries and the odor of guano can be overpowering!

Between these two islands and the Pineda Causeway the flat continues and can be excellent at any time for reds of all sizes. Baby tarpon will work this shoreline during the summer, and the occasional brute will be seen rolling in the deeper waters between the edge of the flat and the channel. In the fall months in the deeper waters adjacent to this flat, terns and gulls will often be found over schooling jacks, ladyfish, and seatrout.

This is a long flat and the fish could be anywhere along it (or not there at all) so expect to do a lot of searching when fishing here. The potential payoff makes the investment of time well worth it.

Port Canaveral

Since the tragedy on September 11, trying to fish in the port has become a somewhat of a problem. New security rules are in place. You are not allowed to fish within 25 yards of any dock or docked vessel. When the cruise ships are in the west turning basin, private vessels are not allowed to enter. They are never allowed in the Trident Basin. Don't even think of going in there. You are not allowed to fish near the locks, which always holds snook and jacks. I'm not sure what the status of the middle basin is (no one has pointed any automatic weapons at me in there) but two naval vessels dock there, so I haven't even tried going in. Finally, and saddest of all for the nearshore angler, the entire beach north of the port to well north of Cape Canaveral from the land out to a distance of three miles is closed for security reasons. No longer can you fish Canaveral Bight. The Wave Scan buoy, a well known tripletail magnet, is out of bounds now. Trespassing in the closed area is a Federal offense.

The Port is still worth fishing though. You can run the beach south of the port to your

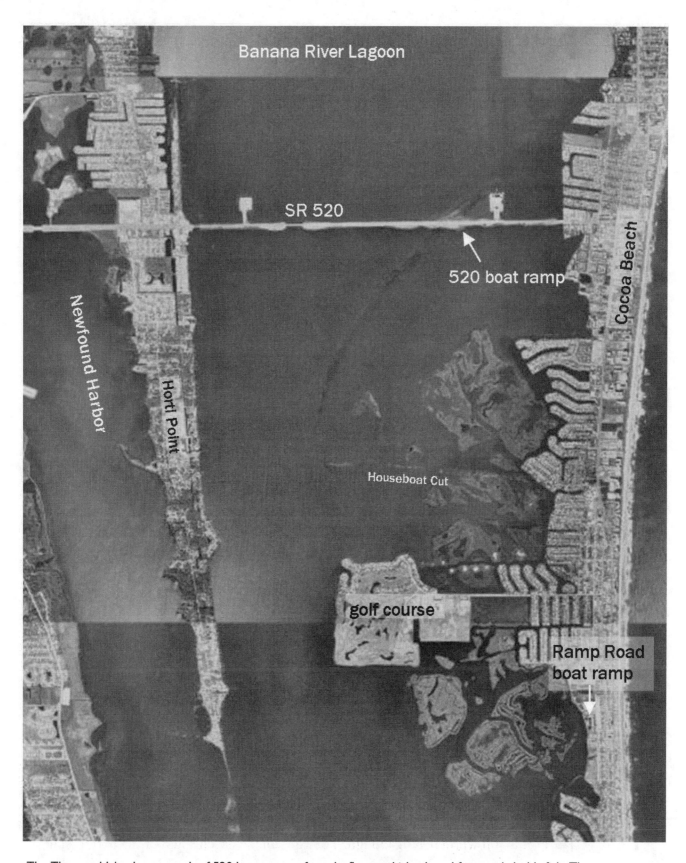

The Thousand Island area south of 520 has a maze of canals, flats, and islands and frequently holds fish. The westside shoreline from 520 south can also be very productive. You could find trophy size redfish anywhere on either side here.

heart's content. You can fish around both jetties. You can fish the buoy line, or go north of the port as long as you stay out at least three miles. There are still plenty of fish to be caught.

In the port itself, night fishing is frequently productive under lighted areas on the south side. You can usually see the fish going off. Jacks, ladyfish, lookdowns and moonfish, and sometimes cutlassfish are the most frequently caught species, but huge old snook live under those docks. How you would get a big snook out of there if you hooked one would be a nice problem to have. I suspect most of the time the fish would win.

Flounder invade the Port in the cooler months, beginning with the mullet run. Finger mullet or mud minnows fished along dropoffs, right on the bottom, will produce for you.

There are lots of mangrove snapper in the port sometimes, and while most are small, there are some very nice ones as well.

The late Don Teddy told me he used to fish with the port with an old man for sheepshead. The gentleman used 20 pound line, a one ounce egg sinker, a #3/0 hook, and fiddler crabs for bait. Although he used a rod and reel, he used it like a cane pole, with the drag locked down all the way. He would fish around the plentiful pilings in the port, and catch sheepshead to six and seven pounds, very entertaining and excellent eating.

The port has a run of weakfish during the winter. They average two to three pounds, and again provide some excellent eating.

The port still has a lot of fishing left. Don't give up on it.

Photo 11- Indian River Lagoon- SR 528 Causeway to the Pineda Causeway

Overview

Some years, this relatively lightly fished stretch of the Indian River Lagoon is one of my favorite summer fishing spots. Snook, reds, trout, tarpon, jacks, and ladyfish will all attack well presented lures in this stretch. Other summers nothing shows up in here. I always find it strange how the fishing varies so greatly from year to year.

One wonderful thing about this stretch (at least as I write this) is that the manatee zones present all around the rest of Brevard County haven't arrived here yet.

Another nice thing about this piece of water is that at its northern end the water stays clear most of the time. You can usually sight fish in here.

Like the areas to the north and south, the shorelines here are fairly straight, have lots of residences, and are lined with docks. Dock fish can be had all year long.

Access

-West side:

-Lee Wenner Park in Cocoa, on the southwest side of SR 520, is a wonderful facility.

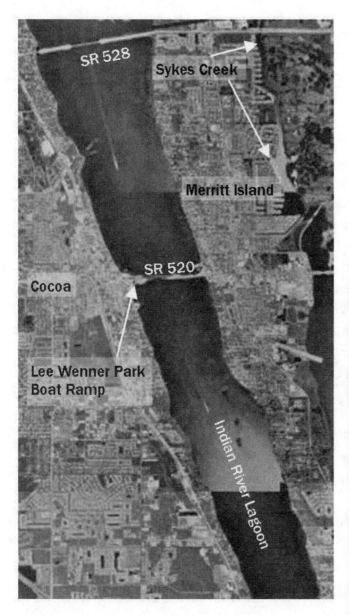

Photo left:
The Indian River Lagoon between 528 and 520 has residential docks lining both sides. There are many good ones. This area is relatively lightly fished, yet can be very productive for snook, trout, redfish, and baby tarpon. Jacks, ladyfish, and other fishes can also be found here.

Sykes Creek is not mentioned in the text, nor is the Barge Canal. Both hold snook though, especially around shoreline structures such as docks. Again, other fish will be found here.

Photo right:
This stretch of the lagoon around Rockledge is lined by homes on both sides. Lots of docks hold fish through here. Due to lots of non-point pollution from lawns, storm drains, etc., water quality here is frequently poor, especially during the summer months. This area is lightly fished, and could be a gold mine to the person who learns it well.

-The Sun Cove Crab House in Pineda has a small ramp and limited parking.

-Pineda Landing, just north of the Pineda Causeway, has a small dirt ramp with limited parking.

There are no ramps on the east side in this stretch.

Fishing Here, West Side

From 528 south, docks line the river bank. I have seen and caught redfish, trout, and snook along this entire stretch, but have done best between 528 and 520. There are some very good docks here. South of the condos that are just south of 520 is another good stretch of docks.

By Pineda there is a canal that runs parallel to this shoreline which holds trout in the winter and tarpon in the summer. Between here and the causeway the shoreline is as irregular as it gets in this stretch, and it frequently holds both trout and redfish.

The Pineda bridge pilings are a good place to try some vertical jigging with a DOA TerrorEyz. Keep the lure down, bumping the bottom. Do not try this with wimpy tackle!

Fishing Here- East Side

Yes, docks here can provide excellent fishing. Between 528 and 520 there are some excellent docks. Also in here is a stand of large Australian pines. When the wind blows from the east these trees shelter this shoreline, making it fishable when a lot of other places are not. You can find snook, trout, reds, tarpon, and jacks, and I have also seen pompano under some docks.

South of 520, I have seen tarpon rolling between docks during the summer, close to 520. Trout and reds use the docks the entire distance to the Pineda Causeway, especially during the winter. Between markers 77 and 79 there are some spoil islands, on the north side of which is a dredged channel which holds winter trout.

The fact is, there aren't a lot of fishermen who fish this stretch, and I don't personally know any who do. It is probably worth investing some time and getting to know. During the week you would usually have the entire place to yourself.

Photo 12- Indian River Lagoon and Banana River Lagoon- Pineda Causeway to Melbourne Causeway

Overview

Both banks of the Indian River Lagoon in this stretch, and of the Banana River Lagoon as well, are developed with residences, some of which ought to be tourist destinations on their own. This means there are lots of docks through here. As always, the best docks are dilapidated structures with at least 18 or 20 inches of water beneath them. Deep water nearby is always a plus. The shorelines are fairly featureless with a few exceptions.

The Banana River Lagoon and the Indian River Lagoon join together just north of the Eau Gallie Causeway at Dragon Point, the southern tip of Merritt Island. The large concrete dragon that used to be a landmark here collapsed recently. The dragon sat on a large rock ledge.

The east side of the Banana River Lagoon south of the Pineda Causeway is paralleled by a canal system locally called the Grand Canal. For those with electric motors this canal system offers fishing all year long, even in the worst weather.

Just south of the Eau Gallie Causeway on the west shoreline of the Indian River Lagoon the Eau Gallie River enters the Indian River Lagoon. On the east side of the lagoon in this stretch are a couple of large points and a couple of small canals.

In general the water quality through here is not as good as in some other areas of the Indian River Lagoon. Non-point runoffs from roads and lawns make the water more turbid than in the north end of the lagoon. Fish definitely still live here. You'll just have to settle for casting to structure more often than casting to sighted fish.

Access

-On the west side of the Indian River Lagoon just north of the Pineda Causeway is a small dirt ramp with limited parking available.

-Also on the west side of the Indian River Lagoon on the Eau Gallie River in Melbourne is Ballard Park, an excellent Brevard County facility.

-Again on the west side of the Indian River Lagoon there is a private ramp at the Intracoastal Marina just off of US 1. Their phone number is 321.725.0090.

-Just south of the Melbourne Causeway on the west side of the Indian River Lagoon is another excellent public ramp.

-There is a public ramp on the southeast side of the Eau Gallie Causeway, hard to use with a strong south wind.

Fishing Here, West Side of Indian River Lagoon

As already stated, the shorelines here have homes on them so there are a lot of residential docks. These docks can hold trout and reds at any time. Snook and baby tarpon can be found during the summer. As always, older docks with lots of growth on them are best, especially with reasonably deep water under them and deeper water nearby. During the summer fishing at night or early in the morning will be most productive.

Jacks may cruise this shoreline in packs during the summer, terrorizing any baitfish that get in their way.

The mouths of Otter Creek and Horse Creek may hold fish, especially if there's some water moving there.

The Pineda Causeway bridge itself shouldn't be ignored. Vertical jigging with DOA TerrorEyz along the pilings can turn up all manner of fish. This is also true at the Eau Gallie and Melbourne Causeways.

Just south of the Eau Gallie Causeway is the mouth of the Eau Gallie River. Trout can be found at the mouth of this creek. Tarpon, snook, and jacks may be inside of it during the summer months. Actually, tarpon may be found anywhere through this entire area during the summer. They tend to follow bait schools. If there are a lot of menhaden in the lagoon you can be sure some large tarpon will be nearby.

South of the river mouth the next large structure is the seawall at the Intracoastal Marina. Deeper water by this wall offers a refuge for redfish and seatrout in both summer and winter months.

Just north of the Melbourne Causeway is a dredge hole, where trout can be found during cold spells in the winter.

Indian River Lagoon, East Side

From Pineda Causeway to Dragon Point the shoreline is solid with docks. The same fish that always use docks will use these. At Dragon Point itself, rocks will attract snook, snapper, and other species of fish. Rocks are rare in these parts.

South of the Eau Gallie Causeway are yet more docks. While this is not a particularly productive area, fish use these docks. The canals around the first point to the south will also hold trout and other species, especially during cold weather.

The docks from Wells Point south to Fisherman's Point can hold trout, snook, and other species during the summer months.

Banana River Lagoon

South of the Pineda Causeway there's a flat on the west side of the channel that can hold redfish at any time of year. These are usually slot sized fish. Trout can be there.

There's a small canal to the west of marker 6 that can hold trout during cold weather.

Any of the docks on either side of the river can hold fish, as can the Pineda and Mathers Bridges. Vertical jigging by the pilings with a DOA TerrorEyz is often deadly.

If you don't mind fishing in people's back yards, the Grand Canal system can hold fish of all kinds all through the year. While I don't get back there much I have seen trout, reds, jacks, snook, and tarpon on such forays as I have taken. A trolling motor is an invaluable aid to fishing here, since the water is frequently too deep to pole.

Pineda Causeway

Indian River Lagoon

Banana River Lagoon

Satellite Beach Grand Canal

Dragon Point

Eau Gallie River

boat ramp

Ballard Park Boat Ramp

Indialantic

Eau Gallie Causeway

Intracoastal Marina

Melbourne Causeway

Like the last section, residential docks line both sides of the Indian River Lagoon between the Pineda and Melbourne Causeways. Fish use these docks as protective structure all year long.

The same is true of the Banana River Lagoon through here as well. Additionally, the east side of the Banana River Lagoon has numerous canals which lead back into the Grand Canal. Although it holds fish all year, this canal acts as a thermal refuge during cold snaps during the winter. Lots of fish gang up in here under the right conditions. Tarpon and snook use this waterway all summer long.

All three bridges will hold fish- black and red drum, mangrove snapper, and other assorted passers by. Some time spent vertical jigging under any of these structures could be time well spent.

Photo 13 Melbourne Causeway to Hog Point

Overview

Do we have more docks here? You bet, but there are also other features. Just south of the Melbourne Causeway is Crane Creek, where jacks, snook, tarpon, and trout will be found. South of this about a mile is Turkey Creek. Still farther south on the west shoreline, Goat Creek enters the river. These creek mouths are always good places to look for fish.

Spoil islands are strung like beads along the ICW, providing good fishing spots for boaters and waders alike. Trout are always attracted to structure like this, but jacks, redfish, and sometimes snook and black drum will be seen around them.

The east shoreline is not as developed as the west side. Grass flats and some mangroves are interspersed with the docks along this whole stretch.

We're getting close enough to Sebastian Inlet here that you will see noticeable water movement from tidal influence.

Access

West Side-

-Just south of the Melbourne Causeway is an excellent ramp with plenty of parking.

-There is a public ramp on the south side of Turkey Creek, on Bianca Drive.

There are no ramps through here on the east side of the lagoon.

Fishing Here, West Side

If you launch at Ballard Park, a few minutes spent vertical jigging under the bridge might be well spent. Another good place to try that's very close to the ramp is at the mouth of, and inside of, Crane Creek. Trout might be found here anytime, and snook, tarpon, and crevalle are the usual summer residents. Yet another place to spend a couple minutes is the dredge hole just north of the causeway. Trout move into this hole during cold weather.

Fishing the drop-offs around the spoil islands near the ICW channel is another good bet for some action from trout. Most spoil islands have a sand bar extending to the west. These bars usually hold bait, and are often good places to try for trout, snook, jacks, and ladyfish. This is true all through this stretch, and all the way to Sebastian Inlet.

The mouth of Turkey Creek could offer trout action at any time of year. If you move into the creek, under the US 1 bridge into the marina basin, tarpon and snook are strong possibilities during the summer months. Try to fish here early and late in the day, or at night.

Moving south, Rocky Point and the mouth of Goat Creek can offer good fishing for trout. Jacks, ladyfish, and the occasional snook will help keep you busy.

Fishing Here, East Side

The shoreline docks from the Melbourne Causeway south to Fisherman's Point often fish well. The next point south, Crab Point, has some canals which hold trout during the winter

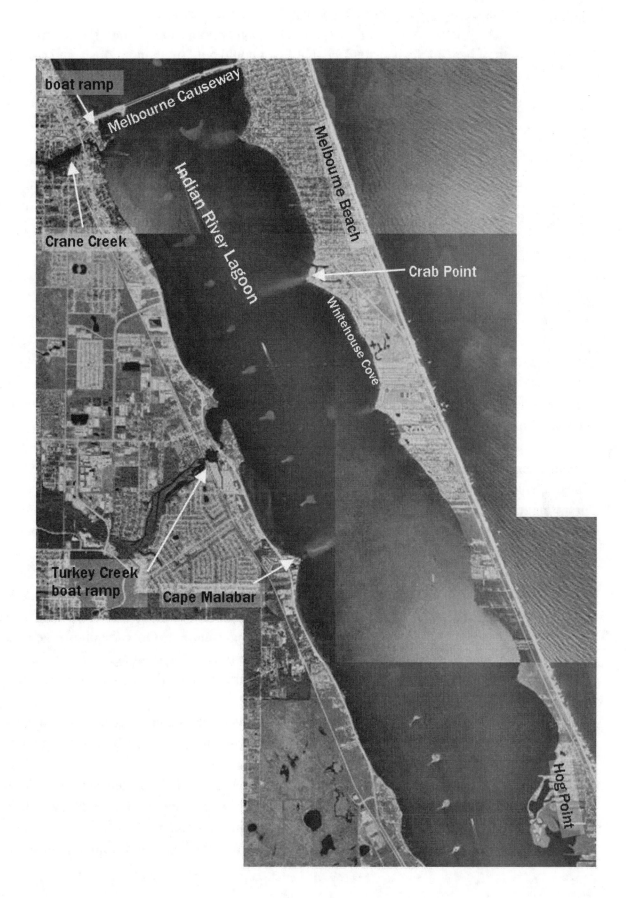

months. The mouths of these canals should be given special attention.

The docks just to the south of Crab Point frequently hold snook. Grass flats along the shoreline south of here all the way to Cocoanut Point could hold trout and redfish, and crevalle will rip bait in here in the summer.

South of Cocoanut Point you will see two markers which designate a cut that goes right into someone's yard. This cut is structure, and there is a dock and some pilings in the water here. This is a good area that can produce trout and snook, and sometimes redfish. The entire area inside of and around Hog Point is one of the better places to fish in this section. The canals will hold tarpon in the summer and sometimes jacks as well. Trout use these canals all year. The canals and the mangrove shorelines will also hold snook, and redfish will use the surrounding flats. Tony DeMao says that outgoing tide in this area is best.

Photo 14- Hog Point to Sebastian Inlet

Overview

The banks of the Indian River Lagoon in this area remain mostly developed, with US 1 running parallel to the west shoreline and SR A1A along the east side. The east side tends to be somewhat less developed than the west. Mangrove islands and grass beds characterize much of the east side, while residential docks line much of the west side. This is only a generalization, as certainly there are plenty of docks along the east side.

Non-point runoff from lawns and storm drains adversely affect water clarity through much of this stretch, particularly during the summer months. Sebastian Inlet does provide a considerable flushing effect, and the water quality close to the inlet is frequently superior to that in the lagoon just a few miles to the north.

Spoil islands line the ICW channel, providing excellent fishing opportunities for both waders and boaters regardless of wind direction. You can camp on many of these islands.

According to Capt. Terry Parsons, you need to use different strategies as the seasons change in order to be consistently successful in this section of the Indian River Lagoon. Terry prefers using artificials, but says that during the summer trout key in on pigfish. Fishermen not using those grunty little fish for bait will not get many big trout then. Once the pigfish get too big, around the middle of August, surface plugs begin to interest the trout again. During the fall mullet run and again in the spring Terry prefers using surface lures. During winter a jig is his lure of choice.

The Sebastian River is the largest feeder stream into the Indian River Lagoon along the entire Space Coast. Many species of fish can be caught here, and it is usually fishable in almost any weather condition.

In the opinion of many, Sebastian Inlet is the finest snook hole in the state. Redfish, tarpon, seatrout, jacks, snapper, flounder, bluefish, and more are all drawn to this fish magnet. No matter what the season, Sebastian Inlet is probably holding some fish.

The Atlantic here provides superb fishing, both from the beach and from near shore

Indian River Lagoon

Pam's Cove

Goat Creek

Hog Point

Washburn Cove

Gibbs Point

Snag Harbor

Grant Public Boat Ramp

Honest Johns Canals

Grant Farm Island

boats. Available species during the summer and fall include large tarpon, snook, redfish, king and Spanish mackerel, little tunny (called bonito locally), big jacks, 'cudas, and sharks.

Access

There is wading access along the west side of the lagoon from US 1. You may have to explore all of the little turnoffs along the road to find the best places. Along SR A1A, wading access is available at Long Point Park and south of Sebastian Inlet.

For boaters, on the west side of the lagoon ramps are located in Grant at the Grant Town Ramp off of US 1; and at Micco Marina ($), about a quarter mile west of US 1 on Main Street in Micco (just north of the US 1 bridge over the Sebastian River).

On the east side of the river, boat ramps are found at Honest Johns Fish Camp ($) off Mullet Creek Road; at Long Point Park ($) on Long Point Road, and at Sebastian Inlet State Park ($).

There are two ramps on Indian River Drive in Sebastian, both of which are free as of this writing. One is at the Sebastian Yacht Club, the other at the end of Main Street.

Fishing- West Side

As mentioned in the overview, the west side has many, many residential docks. Some of these docks consistently hold fish- reds, snook, and trout year-round, and sometimes baby tarpon during the warmer months. The best docks usually look pretty dilapidated, and will have at least 18 or 20 inches of water under them. The less used they look, and the deeper the water, the more likely they are to consistently hold fish. Brand new docks, docks with rod holders and castnets on them, or docks with very little water under them, are less likely to produce for you. Docks with lights on them can be very successfully fished at night, all year long.

Spoil islands north of the inlet usually have bars that come off the islands, extending towards the west shoreline. These bars usually hold bait. If there is any current running they can be excellent places to look for trout, jacks, ladyfish, and sometimes snook.

During the warmer months all of the creek mouths and culverts along the west side will hold snook and baby tarpon, especially after it rains. Goat Creek and the Sebastian River are two prime examples. More will be said about the Sebastian River in a moment.

Jacks in the 10 to 25 pound range will run up the west shoreline of the Indian River Lagoon all summer long, terrorizing baitfish and shredding the tackle of any anglers who get in their way. They will pulverize any type of surface lure. Lead them a good distance and work the lure to make as much commotion as you can.

Terry Parsons tells me that during the summer, redfish will tail in ankle deep (or less!) water along the west shoreline before sunrise, if there is a light west wind. These fish are very spooky and you have to wade for them, since no boat has a shallow enough draft. Terry's favorite lure for this work is a one-eighth ounce Johnson Minnow with a twisty tail threaded onto the hook. He finds these fish by driving along US 1 and stopping and looking at every turnout along the lagoon.

I used to fish the Sebastian River a lot for baby tarpon (to 30 pounds or so) during the summer months. They are always there then. While I always found live or dead finger mullet to be the most effective bait, flies like divers and streamers and lures like Bagley's Finger Mullet, and the DOA Shrimp, Bait Buster, and TerrorEyz were also effective. Snook, seatrout, jacks, sharks, black drum, redfish, ladyfish, lots of hardhead and sail catfish, gar, largemouth bass, and more can all be caught in there. My own best fishing was always west of the railroad trestle up to the closed section of the North Fork, but the South Fork has its fans.

Eric Davis says that early morning will always produce better for Sebastian River tarpon. He adds that during the heat of the day, or during the summer months, snook often hold in the shade of the railroad bridge. Docks along the river also provide good shelter for snook.

If you haven't fished Sebastian River before and tarpon are your quarry the best strategy is to find rolling fish and then fish there. After a while you learn that whether or not the fish are rolling they are there anyway. Just fish at your favorite spots and enjoy the day.

Fishing- East Side

Tony DeMao says that sight fishing is usually possible along this side of the river, except sometimes during the summer. Sight fishing targets will include trout, redfish, snook, and tarpon. Trout tend to be best at the edge of the grass flat, where the water drops off slightly. An outgoing tide and north wind providing the best fishing. Snook prefer deeper water against mangrove shorelines or docks. Reds could be anywhere on the flat, and tarpon will tend to be in water of two feet or more. Every point on this side will hold fish, especially during the mullet run. The bait run does tend to concentrate the fish.

Grass flats run from the Ten Island area (Honest Johns Canals) all the way to the inlet. The current forms cuts through the grass. The fish frequently lie in those cuts. If weather permits, sight fishing is possible. Drift fishing can also be effective.

Summer tarpon are particularly fond of canals such as those at Hog Point and the Honest Johns Canals. If tarpon are high on your must catch list, every canal along this shoreline deserves to be checked, at least during the summer months.

Snook are also frequently found in these canals. During the winter a few years back a seventeen pound plus trout was caught from the Honest Johns Canals. The fisherman, unaware of what he had, filleted and ate what would have been a new all-tackle world record.

Many docks line this side of the lagoon between the Honest Johns area and Long Point. These are also good summer snook haunts. They usually fish better on an outgoing tide.

For those who prefer to fish while drifting, Terry Parsons says that the east side has a few excellent areas for using this technique. You will find an area (the "Old Channel") marked by numerous PVC pipes, known locally as the North Clam Lease, east of channel marker 51. Try to set up a long wind drift here between the shallows and the channel, and cast either surface plugs or jigs.

On the lagoon side of Sebastian Inlet are numerous sand bars with deeper cuts running through them. This is another excellent drift area, especially during the cooler months. The variety of fish here can be amazing. Terry says that his fishermen frequently get 10 or 12 different species while casting jigs here during the winter, and they have gotten as many as 15. Terry said, "During the winter you can get a trout slam: spotted seatrout, silver seatrout, and the true northern weakfish."

Slightly out of our coverage area, the clam lease just west of Black Point (the first large point on the south side of the inlet) is a good place to look for tailing redfish. During the winter, trout will lay up on sandy patches through here and sun themselves.

Fishing- The Inlet

Fishing the inlet, whether from the jetties or from a boat, requires a special breed of angler who is immune to crowds, fish hogs, lawbreakers, rudeness, and mayhem. I am not this type of angler and so avoid the inlet like the plague, but it is a very popular place to fish because of the large numbers of fish that come through. The inlet holds snook almost all year, and at other times tarpon, redfish, flounder, bluefish, jacks, ladyfish, Spanish mackerel, and more pass by. I have been at the inlet when it was really going off, and even though I didn't like the crowds, I have to admit that it was tremendously exciting!

For the landlubber fisherman, there is a short jetty on the inlet's south side, and a much longer jetty on the north side. Catwalks are found under the SR A1A bridge, and shoreline fishing is available for all of the length of the south side and all but the westernmost end of the north side.

Boaters can of course fish anywhere, but conflicts frequently arise between boaters and shoreline or jetty fishermen. The land-bound anglers feel that the boater can go anywhere, and they frequently toss large lead weights at the boaters. Be forewarned.

Another factor any boater needs to be aware of is that the currents run very swiftly through the inlet, especially during full and new moon spring tides. An outgoing tide on an east wind will throw up eight and ten foot swells at the east end of the inlet. Lots of large vessels use the inlet and they throw up large wakes. Many people have died trying to fish here, so be REAL careful. I saw a man and his wife in a small plastic Bass Tracker out in the inlet one day, and quite frankly I was stunned by his stupidity.

The best snook fishing spots are at the ends of the jetties, where the fish are most concentrated. You could get snook anywhere in the inlet, but the jetty ends are the most consistent.

Different folks use different techniques. Many people use large swimming plugs or heavy jigs to fish here. Bait fishing with jumbo shrimp, mullet, mojarras, or other baitfish is also a popular and effective technique.

Fishing at night is usually much more effective than during the daytime. Since there are a lot of rocks down below, bring plenty of terminal tackle. And since the fish are frequently large and the currents are strong, be sure to use heavy enough gear. A 20 pound spinning outfit is not too much! Boaters can either anchor and throw plugs, or drift with bait. Although the snook like the ends of the jetties, they are frequently found on the north side of the north of the north jetty. Snook can also be caught along the beach by going in either direction from the inlet.

Long Point

SR A1A

Sebastian Inlet

Indian River Lagoon

Coconut Point

state park boat ramp

Sebastian Inlet is widely regarded as the best snook hole in the state. Tarpon, jacks, bluefish, redfish, flounder, mangrove snapper, and other species also make forays into this fish magnet.

Since the area around the jetties gets so crowded it takes a certain personality type to fish the inlet itself. But near shore fishing opportunities here are also rich and varied, from tarpon, snook, and redfish to sharks of all kinds and sizes to king mackerel and little tunny and more. Fishing inside the inlet, on the Indian River Lagoon side, also has a lot to offer. Terry Parsons' anglers frequently catch 12 or more species in one day here.

Capt. Tony DeMao says, "Night fishing through this stretch is often very productive, right up into Melbourne. The best places to fish are lighted docks, and the closer the light is to the water the better the dock will usually fish. Weather is important though- you don't want any wind. Wind puts the fish off for some reason. Outgoing tide is definitely best. These docks often hold really big sheepshead.

Once it starts to get light you'll often see big tarpon rolling out near or in the ICW channel. They don't like water less than about five feet deep. You'll have to fish these fish early in the day. Once the sun gets up they'll still be there but they stay down deep. You can't effectively use artificials then."

Fishing- The Ocean

You allowed me to pontificate at great lengths in an earlier chapter about nearshore fishing. This type of fishing reaches its pinnacle here outside of Sebastian Inlet.

According to Terry Parsons, during the summer months tarpon, sharks, king mackerel, and big jack crevalle can all be caught by slow trolling with mullet, menhaden, greenies, or large plugs. Tarpon can often be sight fished as well with all kinds of tackle, including fly rods. Terry often gets his biggest fish quite close to the beach, including giant redfish.

Little tunny are sometimes found in large schools busting on the surface, superb sport on fly or light tackle. Many times where there are tunny, big barracudas will also be found. Anytime you go out of the inlet you need to be ready for anything.

The ocean fishing peaks during the mullet run. Live bait works, but Parsons likes plugsbig ones. A former surfcaster from New Jersey, Terry hasn't forgotten his roots in spite of his nearly 30 years of fishing here. He likes big Atom poppers during the run, plugs of three or four ounces. He frequently tosses these from the beach, and held the Florida state redfish record with a 50 pound class fish that he caught while doing this. Big sharks and tarpon also fall for this.

In Conclusion

You've reached the end of my text. Thank you! I hope it has been and will continue to be helpful to you. I guide in much of the area covered in this book, so if you want more direct information, I'm just a phone call or a charter away. Also, please feel free to visit my website. The URL is www.spottedtail.com.

Thanks again, and best of luck in your fishing adventures along Florida's Space Coast!

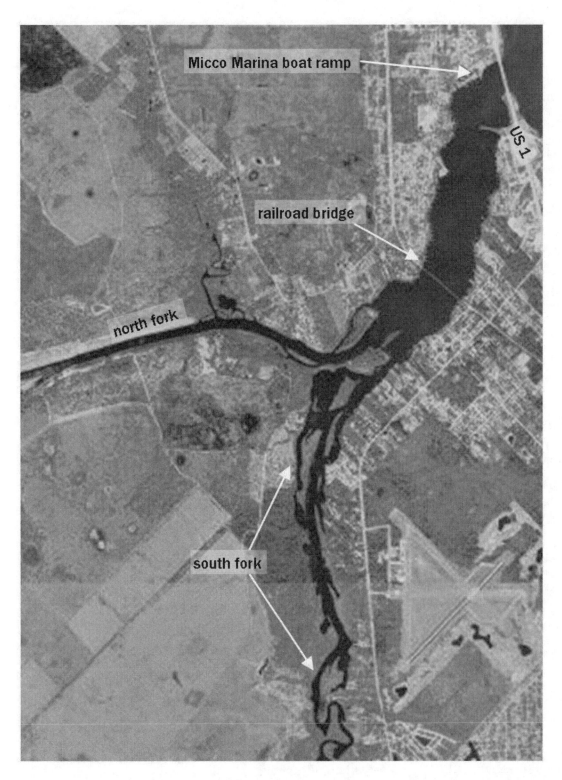

Sebastian River offers a protected place to fish when the weather is less than perfect, and offers quite a fishery in its own right. Bridges and riverside docks hold snook, and tarpon to about 30 pounds can be found rolling all through the river all summer long. Jacks, ladyfish, sharks, and other species will sometimes be found here.

The entire Sebastian River west of the US 1 bridge is a slow speed manatee zone.

Index

Index of Aerial Photographs

ARGONAUT PUBLISHING COMPANY
284 Clearview Road
Chuluota, FL 32766
(407) 977-5207
spottedtail@spottedtail.com
www.spottedtail.com

A Sample SPECIAL REPORT by Captain John Kumiski ©2000
Created especially for <u>**Your Name Here!**</u>

How to Find and Catch Redfish at the Merritt Island National Wildlife Refuge!

Vast areas of crystal clear water cover much of Florida's Merritt Island National Wildlife Refuge (MINWR), surrounding the Kennedy Space Center, one hour's drive east of Orlando. These waters, the south end of the Mosquito Lagoon and the north end of the Indian River Lagoon, shelter large numbers of redfish, fish that regularly top 20 pounds in weight. You want to catch these fish, but don't know quite where to start. This Special Report tells you how to do it!

EQUIPMENT

One thing that anyone attempting to catch these fish absolutely must have in order to be successful is the right equipment and a plan for using it. Topping the list of necessities are a wide brimmed hat and good polarized sunglasses with brown or dark amber lenses. Under the best of conditions seeing these fish is relatively easy; however, don't expect great conditions all the time! Without these hat and glasses your chances will usually be poor.

If you will be wading, wear wading shoes to protect your feet from rocks and other bottom debris. Always use sunscreen to protect your skin from an often blistering Florida sun. Finally, the Mosquito Lagoon wasn't given its name on a whim. Carry an effective insect repellant or be prepared to suffer the consequences, especially at dawn and dusk.

You can choose either fly or spin tackle. Both types of tackle have certain distinct advantages. While sight fishing, a spin fisherman can have his lure on its way to spotted fish within a second of seeing them, without the need to false cast. He can react faster. But a relatively heavy spinning lure hits the water with a heavy splash compared to a fly, and that splashdown can spook an entire school of wary fish. Flies may take a couple seconds longer to get there, but the presentation is much quieter and so oftentimes it's more effective.

Depending on wind conditions, fly fishermen could use any rod between a six- and nine-weight. A quality reel with at least 150 yards of backing is a must. The fish average a fairly large size (10 pounds) and once hooked they will scream line off in a hurry. Use a weight-forward floating line. Long leaders are preferred, between 9 and 12 feet depending on wind conditions, tapered down to a 12 or 15 pound tippet.

Fly selection need not be complicated. Carry weighted and unweighted flies in sizes 4, 2, and 1. Make sure some are light in color and others are dark. You could get by with only four patterns in most redfishing situations- the seaducer in yellow and grizzly, deerhair poppers for blindcasting while wading, Clouser minnows in chartreuse and white and brown and white, and some small crab patterns for tailing fish.

Spin fishermen need a six to seven foot light action rod, a good quality reel packed with eight pound test, and a similarly small lure selection. Weedless gold spoons such as the Johnson minnow (1/8-1/2 oz), a surface plug like the 7M Mirrolure, the shallow running DOA BaitBuster, the DOA Shrimp, and soft plastic baits like the Rip-Tide Jerk Baits or Bass Assassin which can be rigged weedless, in both light and dark colors, will cover all needs.

Plug casters will use comparable equipment.

Tying a Bimini twist in the end of the line and then attaching a short piece of 15-20 pound fluorocarbon as a shock leader is a good idea. Regardless of what type of tackle you use, be sure to bring enough lures. You'd hate to run out of the "hot" lure if you lost a couple due to breakoffs!

TECHNIQUES

Summertime fishing anywhere in Florida is usually an early morning proposition, and the MINWR is no exception. The sun heats up the water and by mid-afternoon most shallow flats are too hot for the fish. Afternoon thunderstorms can make the flats a dangerous place to be. So plan to fish as soon as it is light enough to see.

During the spring and fall the fish will feed on the flats any time of day, as long as anglers in boats aren't running the flats making a fuss. It gets windy this time of year and if the water gets muddy the game is up. But if the weather is good the fishing can be tremendous. Fall is off season and you may have the entire flat to yourself.

During the winter the weather is critical. If the sun is out and the wind is negligible, fishing can absolutely boggle the mind. Redfish come into shallow water to sun themselves, sometimes in large schools. Wading anglers can pick off fish after fish. If there is sunshine the late afternoon is the best time of day to fish since the water will be warmest then. If you fish the lee shoreline you will find fish tailing in the afternoon well into the evening until it's too dark to see. They can be caught easily by fly fishermen using crab patterns or by conventional tackle anglers using soft plastic baits.

In both the Indian River and the southern Mosquito Lagoon there are no tides. Wind direction therefore is the dominant factor in determining the movement of fish. Although there is no hard and fast rule the fish usually move into the wind. So by "going with the flow" while fishing, casts to fish will generally be head-on shots- the most effective kind. If you can have the sun at your back, seeing those fish will be much easier.

If you must fish during the day in the summer, start as early as possible and work out deeper on the flat. Cooler water here will allow the fish a degree of comfort they would not have otherwise. The situation is reversed during the winter. The sun warms up the shallows enough to allow the fish to use it. They come in to feed during the later part of the day unless weather conditions are absolutely perfect.

You must decide whether to wade or to use a boat. The wader has the advantage of stealth on his side. He can get much closer to the fish. There is the aesthetic of being in the fish's element. It's cooler in the summer. But waders are restricted to shallower areas and cannot cover nearly as much water as a boating angler.

Anglers in boats will scare more fish, but they can see a lot better and usually will have shots at many more. You can search a lot of water in a boat, looking for a large school of fish if you prefer, instead of working on the occasional single or pair.

Whether you are wading or fishing from a skiff, slowly move with either the sun (first choice) or the wind at your back looking for anything which might be a redfish. If there are no fish visible, blind casting will often produce a few. Just cast all around, keying on breaks between the sand and grass on the bottom, or cast to schools of bait if present.

If you can see fish, either cruising, tailing, or pushing wakes make your casts fall a few feet in front of the fish, letting the lure sink to the bottom if necessary. The lure should never move toward the fish, but should rather appear to be escaping from it. As soon as you think they're close enough to see it, move it slowly while watching the fish.

If they see it there will be no doubts about it. They do one of three things- flee in abject terror, come check it out and refuse it, or come check it out and eat it. If they flee, the lure was fouled with grass, or moved at them, or was too close to them before it moved. If they refuse it, check the lure. If it is not fouled with grass or algae, change to a different color or different type. If they eat it, set the hook.

If you see fish pushing up a wake, cast several feet ahead of it and move the lure SLOWLY. Sometimes when the fish are pushing a wake, they are swimming fast, with an obvious agenda, and aren't interested in eating. If they don't strike don't let this bother you. Tailing fish are eating, though. With spin tackle a lure like the DOA Standard Shrimp that doesn't make a huge splash when it hits the water is a good choice. Fly tackle actually works better for tailing fish since the fly hits the water so delicately.

With spin tackle put the lure a foot or two ahead of the fish. You want the splash to be heard but not threatening. Hopefully the fish will come to investigate, see the shrimp (just barely TWITCH it) and eat it.

Flies can be put closer to the fish. A Clouser minnow, or a small Merkin crab fly made from wool, or my Fuzzy Crab pattern, are good choices. These flies hit the water with a soft, seductive "splat", sink rapidly into the feeding zone, and perfectly imitate a favorite redfish food. Crab flies don't even need to be moved. If the fish sees it and wasn't spooked by the presentation they'll usually eat it immediately.

Fly fishermen now must clear the line. If it fouls on anything the leader will instantly break, you'll have a super adrenaline rush, and will be out the fly. Once the fish is on the reel, and for spin or plug fishermen also, extend the rod into the air. Let the fish run.   Let the fish go. If you try to stop it he'll break off. With any type of tackle, make sure the drag is not set too tightly.

After that first run is over he will take a couple more shorter ones. Reds will also rub their snout in the bottom trying to dislodge the hook. Once you've beaten him, will you be keeping or releasing him?

Redfish have rather strict laws protecting them. They must be released if they are less than 18" (uncommon in these waters) or larger than 27".

If you'll be releasing it, handle the fish gently. Leave him in the water if possible. If not, hold the fish parallel to the water's surface and belly up. They have small teeth which can cut you if you "lip" it like you would a largemouth bass, unless you wear a glove. Spines on dorsal and ventral fins can stick you, too. So handle with care! Remove the lure (barbless hooks are recommended), revive him until he can swim away, and release him to grow and thrill another fisherman. And congratulations to you!

All of the above supposes that you have good visibility. But if you're fishing early/late in the day, or if it is overcast, or if you are not used to looking for fish, seeing these fish in the water can be very difficult. They can still be caught. All other things being equal, the fish will be on their favorite flats feeding when weather conditions allow it. If you're there too you might just get a couple.

When you use this blind casting technique for redfish lure choice is important. You want a lure with which you can cover a lot of water reasonably quickly. With spinning or plug tackle a popper is the lure of choice. The noise the plug makes attracts the fish to it. With fly tackle the deerhair (or other) popper works well for the same reason.

Search the water you can see into for fish. If you see any, cast to them! There's no sense in turning down any good opportunities.

Keep your lure in the water into which you cannot see. Generally this will be in the deeper water, but fish are in there. Keep casting into this water and retrieving your lure. Fish every cast as if you expect to hook a fish. Sooner or later you will!

Make long casts. You'll cover more water this way, giving more fish the chance to see your offering. Also, oftentimes the fish will follow your lure or fly for quite a distance before finally making up their mind. Long retrieves give them the opportunity to do this.

Of course once you hook up, play the fish as explained above.

WHERE to GO- Boaters

In the Indian River south of the Haulover Canal the flats off Black Point and Dummit Creek (east side of river) consistently produce fish. The creek itself often hold fish.

North of the canal the fish can be found anywhere along either side of the river all the way up to the end of the lagoon, north of Scottsmoor. Lush grass beds and clear water are indications that fish may be there. Bait, usually in the form of finger mullet, is another good sign. Stingrays may or not be helpful, as these redfish almost never follow rays like they do in south Florida.

In the Mosquito Lagoon, the large flat across from (east side) and to the north of the Haulover Canal is an excellent place to start. The west side of the lagoon south of the canal and south of the remains of the Lightning Research Station (look for pilings in the water leading out from a small parking lot on shore)is another consistent producer.

At the south end of the lagoon, fish may be anywhere around Pelican Island. They were tailing here all through the winter last year. The large flat out in front of Pelican Island is known as the Middle Flat. At its northern end, a school of reds can sometimes be found. This school contains hundreds of individuals.

Remember that due to the lack of tidal flow in this system there is no way to predict the location of fish anywhere with any accuracy. They must be hunted down, since they tend to travel constantly. If there are no fish where you start looking, try somewhere else.

WHERE to GO- Waders

Waders don't have the same freedom of movement, but they can still try several different areas in one day. If you are approaching the refuge from Titusville, continue east on SR 402 until you reach the traffic light at the intersection of SR 3. Turn left and head north for about three miles. You are looking for a small sign on the right hand side of the road which says "NASA Atmospheric Sciences". Take a right here. At the fork in the road go right. You will find yourself on a dike road on the west side of the Mosquito Lagoon.

During the winter and spring you can actually see fish tailing at the water's edge sometimes. The bottom of the lagoon here is a little soft but all of it is wadable. There is a two mile stretch of this road which is separated from the lagoon by a ditch. UNDER NO CIRCUMSTANCES SHOULD YOU TRY TO CROSS ANY DITCH!!

One other hazard to mention. Right along the shoreline in a few place there are muck pockets. If you step into one you will sink. This is a little scary and quite messy but I've never had any trouble extricating myself from one. If you test to see if the bottom will support your weight and it doesn't, back up and try again 20' away or so.

Waders need primarily to keep blindcasting, as seeing fish when you are so close to the water is tough. In the cooler parts of the year the fish will get in VERY skinny water when the wind is down and cruise or tail- an obvious advantage to you. If there are no fish present, or if there's a screaming east wind, try a different spot.

Drive out the way you came in. When you reach SR 3, take a left and the take a right on the first dirt road you come to, only a couple hundred yards. This road will take you back to Dummit Cove. A WIDE spot on the dirt road which obviously looks like a parking spot marks the cove. Identification is further enhanced by the culverts which go under the road, connecting the mosquito control ditch to the Indian River.

Dummit Cove can look like Sea World, or the Sahara Desert. Wade around for a while looking for visible fish and blindcasting in the meantime. If nothing cooperates after an hour or so, get in the car and try the last spot.

Drive back out to SR 3 the way you drove in and take a left heading north. Cross over the Haulover Canal. A couple of miles after the canal is a lefthand turn onto a dirt road (marked by two eight by eight inch posts) which after only two hundred yards of so comes to the bank of the Indian River. It then turns and runs north along the river for several miles, ending at US 1. This whole shoreline is wadable where you don't have to cross a ditch and often holds fish. If this doesn't work, well- have you considered cutting your lawn???

Boat Ramps

Boat ramps which allow access to the Mosquito Lagoon are at the following locations:
From A1A south of New Smyrna-
-J.B.'s Fish Camp has a ramp. A run south of about two miles will put you into Refuge waters. There is a charge to use this ramp.
-Behind the Visitor's Center just south of the National Seashore entrance there is an excellent ramp.
-Just south of Turtle Mound there is another good ramp.
-Across from Parking Lot 5 there is an unimproved dirt ramp.
Only those with small boats and four-wheel drive vehicles should even attempt this one.
From Playalinda Beach-
-There is a good dirt ramp between Parking Lots 7 and 8 at Playalinda Beach at Eddy Creek.

From the west side of the Lagoon-

-There is a ramp on the Haulover Canal. This one gets crowded on weekends. Keep in mind the entire canal is a slow speed manatee zone. This ramp allows access to both the Indian River and the Mosquito Lagoon.

There are other unimproved ramps along the west side of the lagoon off of S.R. 3. Those with boats 18 feet or larger would be advised not to use them.

The best Indian River access for boaters is the ramp at Parrish Park, on the east side of the Indian River on SR 406. There's a paved ramp, good for small boats only, in Scottsmoor at the end of Huntington Road, off of US 1 several miles north of Titusville.

MEALS AND ACCOMODATIONS

Along US 1 in Titusville are many places to eat and sleep. The best known restaurant in town is the Dixie Crossroads on SR 406, west of US 1. This seafood restaurant specializes in rock shrimp, and almost always has a line of people waiting to get in. The best motel in Titusville is probably the Holiday Inn on US 1 down by SR 50, 321.269.2121. They have special rates for fishermen. Be sure to ask.

There are several other motels on SR 50 by its intersection with I-4, just a few miles away.

RESOURCES

Fly fishers will want to stop at the Fly Fisherman, an excellent full service fly shop on US 1 on the south side of Titusville. Their phone number is (321)267-0348.There are several mom and pop bait and tackle stores in Titusville. Those who prefer big discount stores will find a WalMart at the intersection of I-95 and SR 50.

For those looking for a guide, the author of this Special Report guides on the Indian and Banana Rivers and the Mosquito Lagoon. Captain John Kumiski's phone number is (407) 977-5207, email spotted-tail@spottedtail.com. If he's booked he can recommend other good guides.

CONCLUSION

So you could go to the Merritt Island National Wildlife Refuge and flounder around on your own for a month and never see any redfish. Or you can take the recommendations supplied in this Special Report and catch those reds on your own. Let me know how you do (reach me at 284 Clearview Road, Chuluota, FL 32766, (407) 977-5207, e-mail spottedtail@spottedtail.com, www.spottedtail.com), and good luck!!!
****

NEWS FLASH!!!

The St. John's River Water Management District has been reconnecting the salt marshes behind the dike roads to the lagoon system by placing culverts under the dikes. This work has been going on for the past couple of years and is nearing completion. Redfish, tarpon, snook, and other gamefish have moved through the culverts into the marshes to feed on the plentiful minnows back there. An entire new fishery has opened up, one which I yet to fully investigate. Be the first one on your block to take advantage of this new sport fishing opportunity which has opened on the MINWR!
****

Another, Sadder, News Flash

Due to security concerns raised in the wake of the Spetember 11 tragedy, portions of the Merritt Island National Wildlife Refuge have been closed to all entry: The south end of the Mosquito Lagoon, south from a line connecting the Lightning Research Station on Bio Lab Road to the Observatory at the north end of Playalinda Beach. When these restrictions will be lifted (if ever) is anybody's guess. Trespass in these areas is a Federal offense.

Enjoy a Day or a Week Experiencing the Indian River Lagoon System with Capt. John Kumiski!

We specialize in sight fishing with fly and light tackle for redfish that sometimes exceed 30 pounds, seatrout, snook, tarpon, giant black drum, and more in the waters of the Merritt Island National Wildlife Refuge, an hour's drive east of Orlando and next to the Kennedy Space Center. Catch fish in the shadow of rockets!

Florida's wildlife contributes to an extraordinary angling experience. We observe all kinds of birds including egrets, herons, white and glossy ibis, ospreys, bald eagles, brown and white pelicans, and roseate spoonbills. We see dolphins on almost every trip, and often see manatees and alligators, too.

Fish from a Maverick Mirage 2, an Old Town canoe, or an Ocean Kayak, always your choice.

Fish nearshore Atlantic waters, the Banana River Lagoon, the Indian River Lagoon, or the Mosquito Lagoon, always your choice.

We fish in beautiful, clean waters completely surrounded by protected Federal lands. This lagoon system is a lovely place to spend a day or a lifetime. If you want to catch fish in exquisite surroundings, contact me now at 407.977.5207 or by email at spottedtail@spottedtail.com!

Life is great, I love my work, and **I look forward to fishing with you!**

JOHN KUMISKI has been a U.S. Coast Guard licensed captain and inshore fishing guide for 15 years. He is the author of Fishing the Space Coast, Flyfishing for Redfish, Flyrodding Florida Salt- How and Where to Catch Saltwater Fish on Flies in the Sunshine State, Fishing the Everglades- A Complete Guide for the Small Boater, and Saltwater Fly Fishing. He has had hundreds of magazine articles published about all kinds of fishing in many different magazines, including Florida Sportsman, Salt Water Sportsman, Sport Fishing, Tide, Saltwater Fly Fishing, and others. Some of the organizations he belongs to include the Coastal Conservation Association, the Federation of Fly Fishers, the Florida Outdoor Writers Association, and the Outdoor Writers Association of America. He holds a flycasting instructor certification from the FFF, is currently a two term president of the Indian River Guides Association, and is a two term past president of the Backcountry Flyfishing Association of Altamonte Springs. He teaches fly and light tackle fishing classes at Brevard Community College, and gives slide presentations all over the southeast.

If you'd like more information about charters, John can be reached at 284 Clearview Road, Chuluota, FL 32766, **(407) 977-5207**, or email at spottedtail@spottedtail.com. More information is available on his website at **www.spottedtail.com**.

The Resource Catalog: INFORMATION!
from Argonaut Publishing Company

Books

Fishing the Space Coast- An Angler's Guide (Ponce de Leon Inlet to Sebastian Inlet)
by Capt. John A. Kumiski

Do You Want to Catch Fish on Florida's Space Coast?
This stretch of the Florida's Atlantic Coast and the adjacent Indian River Lagoon system offers world class angling for redfish, black drum, spotted seatrout, tripletail, and more. In addition, snook, tarpon, cobia, Spanish and king mackerel, little tunny, jack crevalle, bluefish, barracuda, sharks, and many other species can be found in these waters at various times of the year. Do you know how to catch them?
This book will make you a better fisherman. You will learn:
*How-to choose rods, reels, lines, lures, baits, rigging, and techniques that work here.
*When to fish. The fishery changes with the seasons. This book will help you adjust your strategies.
*Where to fish. Aerial photographs pinpoint hot spots all along the Space Coast.
Many of the Space Coast's finest fishing guides shared secrets contained in this book, such well known anglers as Eric Davis, Kent Gibbens, Fred Hill, Mike Hakala, Terry Parsons, Rodney Smith, and several more.

Fishing the Space Coast, 120 pp., paperback, $19.95

Flyfishing for Redfish- The Complete Guide to Catching Red Drum on Flies
by Capt. John A. Kumiski

Flyfishing for Redfish will easily teach you how to catch more redfish by sharing these secrets:
-how the fish behave; which tackle and flies to use; how tides affect the fish; how to find and see the fish; how to present your fly so the fish will eat it; tactics for wading and for fishing from a boat; who and where the guides and fly shops are in every state where redfish are found, complete with phone numbers; what flies you need and how to tie them (or where to buy them); and MORE! If you want to catch redfish on fly tackle, then you need this book!

Flyfishing for Redfish, 160 pp., paperback, $19.95

Sport Fish of Florida   by Vic Dunaway

Vic's long needed book identifies 231 species of Florida fishes, everything from billfish to baitfish. All are illustrated in full color and include scientific and common names, distinguishing features, food value, average and record sizes, range throughout Florida, habitats, game qualities, and best fishing methods.

Sport Fish of Florida, 256 pp., paperback, $16.95

124

Vic Dunaway's Complete Book of Bait, Rigs, and Tackle   by Vic Dunaway

This book covers everything that might be implied by the title-spin, plug, and fly tackle, hooks, sinkers, floats, lines, leaders, knots, fishing accessories, and rigging methods for both natural and artificial baits.

Vic Dunaway's Complete Book of Bait, Rigs, and Tackle, 224 pp., paperback, $16.95

Fishing in the Florida Keys and Flamingo   by Stu Apte

Fishing the Florida Keys is the classic where-to book on light tackle fishing in the Florida Keys. If you're thinking of going there, you need it, and that's that. Does Stu have the qualifications to write a book like this? He lived in the Keys for years and was one of the most sought-after professional guides, fishing such other legends as Al McClane and Joe Brooks. He's also held 44 different world records.

        This little gem contains tips from Stu on light tackle fishing, offshore fishing, backcountry know-how, and charts which clearly show where the best fishing spots are. It belongs in every Florida angler's library.

Fishing in the Florida Keys and Flamingo 80 pp., paperback. $7.95

The Florida Atlas and Gazetteer   from DeLorme Mapping

Are you tired of getting lost trying to find those out-of-the way fishing spots? The Florida Atlas and Gazetteer solves your problem! Containing detailed road maps of the entire state, this book is an invaluable resource when finding your way from point A to point B on Florida's highway system is your highest priority.

The Florida Atlas and Gazetteer, 128 pp., paperback. $19.95

-Fishing Maps-

Pasadena Top Spot Fishing Maps pride themselves on making reliable, accurate, waterproof charts with well marked fishing areas. Important information such as the best times of year, types of fish available, artificial fish habitats, and underwater structure are all shown in an easy to read format.

Homosassa area, N-201
-Tampa Bay area, N-202
-Charlotte Harbor area, N-203
-Ten Thousand Islands area, N-204
-Everglades Park area, N-206
-Florida Bay area, N-207
-Middle Keys area, N-208
-Lower Keys area, N-209
-Miami area, N-211
-Fort Lauderdale area, N-212
-Palm Beach area, N-213
-Jupiter to Stuart area, N-214

Fishing Maps, con't.

-Stuart to South Fort Pierce and St. Lucie area, N-215
-Fort Pierce to Vero Beach area, N-216
-Sebastian Inlet and Palm Bay area, N-217
-Cape Canaveral area, N-218
-Mosquito Lagoon area, N-219
-Daytona Beach to Jacksonville area, N-221

Top Spot Maps, $15.95 each

-Special Reports-

Special Reports by Capt. John Kumiski provide the detailed how-to and where-to information you need to step into a new area or situation and fish confidently and successfully. The five page reports are updated constantly. Go to pp. 118 to 122 of this book to see a sample Special Report.

The Keys
-How to Find and Catch Bonefish on Long Key,   SR-LK
-How to Find and Catch Bonefish at Pennekamp State Park,   SR-KL
-Fishing Keys Bridges, SR-KB
-Fishing the Keys from a Houseboat, SR-KH

The Everglades
-How to Find and Catch Fish at Flamingo, Everglades National Park, SR-FF
-Day Trips for Canoeing Anglers from Flamingo, Everglades National Park, SR-CF
-How to Find and Catch Backcountry Snook from Flamingo, Everglades N. P.,   SR-FS
-Fishing The Cape Sable Area, Everglades National Park, SR-CS
-Fishing Chatham Bend, Everglades National Park, SR-CB
-Fishing Lostman's River, Everglades National Park, SR-LR
-Fishing and Canoe Camping the Everglades, SR-EC
-Fishing for Cape Sable Seatrout, SR-ES
-Fishing the Everglades from a Houseboat, SR-EH
-How to Find and Catch Fish in the10,000 Islands, Everglades National Park, SR-TI
-Everglades Tarpon, SR-ET

Jacksonville and Vicinity
-How to Find and Catch Redfish in Nassau Sound, SR-NS
-Fishing for Redfish in Jacksonville's Backcountry, SR-JR
-Fishing Opportunities in Cumberland Sound, SR-OC

East Central Florida
-How to Find and Catch Redfish at the Merritt Island National Wildlife Refuge, SR-M
-Fishing at Ponce Inlet and New Smyrna Beach, Canaveral National Seashore, SR-CN
-Fishing the Banana River Manatee Refuge, SR-MR
-Tactics for Sebastian River Tarpon, SR-SR
-Orlando as a Fishing Destination, SR-OF
-Fly Fishing for Bass and Bream in the Wekiva River, SR-WR

Special Reports, con't

-How to Catch Summer Seatrout in the Mosquito Lagoon, SR-SS
-Floating Florida's Spring Creeks for Bass and Bream, SR-SC
-Fishing the Intracoastal Waterway at Daytona/New Smyrna, SR-DB
-Fishing Opportunities Along Cape Canaveral Beaches, SR-CC
-Fishing Opportunities Along the Jupiter Coast, SR-JF

Southwest Florida
-How to Find and Catch Fish in Bull Bay, Charlotte Harbor, SR-CH
-Fishing Captiva Pass and Redfish Pass, SR-CP
-How to Find and Catch Pine Island Redfish, SR-PI
-Fishing at Cayo Costa State Park, SR-CY
-Southwest Florida's Beach Tarpon Run, SR-BT
-Charlotte Harbor's Winter Snook, SR-WS

West Central Florida
-Fly Fishing for Homosassa Tarpon, SR-HT
-Fishing Opportunities at Cedar Key, SR-CK

Saltwater Fly Fishing
-How to Choose your Fishing Guide, SR-CG
-Constructing Saltwater Fly Rod Leader Systems, SR-LS
-Practical Fly Selection for Florida's Saltwater, SR-SF
-Getting Started in Saltwater Fly Fishing, SR-GS
-A Primer for Waders, SR-PW
-How to Increase Your Ability to See Fish, SR-HS
-How to Fight Big Fish Successfully with Light Tackle, SR-BF
-Fly Fishing for Jack Crevalle, SR-JC
-Getting Started in Tying Flies for Saltwater, SR-FT
-Tying and Using Crab Patterns, SR-UC
-A Guide to Fly Fishing from Canoes, SR-FC

Miscellaneous
-Improve Your Fishing Photography, SR-FP
-Practical Tips for Redfish on the Surface, SR-RT

Special Reports, $6.95 each, or three for $17.95

Shipping Information

If your order is between:	Standard shipping cost is:	Priority shipping cost is:
$1.00 to 30.00	$4.95	$6.95
$30.01 to 65.00	$7.95	$9.95
$65.01 to 100.00	$10.95	$14.95
Over $100.00	No charge	$25.00

Order Form

You can contact us by snail mail, email, telephone, or fax. Please make checks out to:

Argonaut Publishing Company
284 Clearview Road
Chuluota, FL 32766
407.977.5207 (phone and fax)
email: spottedtail@spottedtail.com

If there is no one in the office when you call, please leave a message. Please- speak slowly!
1) Tell us who you are and where you want the order shipped.
2) Tell us what you want to order.
3) Tell how you would like to pay (if by credit card, please leave the number and expiration date).
4) Florida residents, be prepared to pay 7 percent sales tax.
5) Shipping costs depend on what you order and how you want it shipped (see chart on previous page.) Standard shipping is free on orders over $100.00. On in-stock items, orders usually ship the same day or the next day.

Thank you for your business!

Ship to:_____

Street_____

City_____ State_____ Zip_____

Phone_____

Quantity	Description (title and author)	Price	Total

Method of Payment: Credit Card Check Money Order

Credit Card #_____

Expiration Date _____

Signature _____

Merchandise Total	
FL Delivery, add 7% sales tax	
Shipping and Handling (see p. 127)	
Amount Enclosed	